WINCHESTER SCHOOL OF MISSION

07953

Enjoying the Gospel of John

D1513713

Resource Room
Church House
9 The Close
WINCHESTER
SO23 9LS
Tel: 01962 624760

The Bible Reading Fellowship

BRF encourages regular, informed Bible reading as a means of renewal in churches.

BRF publishes three series of regular Bible Reading notes: *New Daylight, Guidelines* and *First Light.*

BRF publishes a wide range of materials for individual and group study. These include resources for Advent, Lent, Confirmation and the Decade of Evangelism.

Write or call now for a full list of publications:

The Bible Reading Fellowship
Peter's Way
Sandy Lane West
Oxford
OX4 5HG
Tel: 0865 748227

The Bible Reading Fellowship is a Registered Charity

ENJOYING THE GOSPEL OF JOHN

A running commentary upon the
self-revelation of the servant of the Lord

R.E.O. WHITE

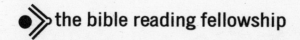

the bible reading fellowship

Text copyright © 1993 R.E.O. White

Published by
The Bible Reading Fellowship
Peter's Way
Sandy Lane West
Oxford
OX4 5HG
ISBN 0 7459 2558 8
Albatross Books Pty Ltd
PO Box 320
Sutherland
NSW 2232
Australia
ISBN 0 7324 0764 8

First edition 1993
All rights reserved

Unless otherwise stated, the Scripture quotations
are from the Revised Standard Version of the Bible
copyright © 1946, 1952, 1971 by the Division of
Christian Education of the National Council of the
Churches of Christ in the USA.

A catalogue record for this book is available
from the British Library

Printed and bound in Great Britain
by Cox & Wyman Ltd, Reading

Contents

EXPLORING THE BOOK

Introduction

In all the world's literature no book of comparable length has provoked so wide, so deep, so well-informed study as the Gospel of John. The following pages attempt to glean only what is positive, clear, illuminating and rewarding from years of pondering possible interpretations, weighing varied arguments, and comparing rival theories. Those who best know this field of study will quickly realize how very much has been omitted. No list of 'acknowledgments' could possibly be adequate, though wide indebtedness is acknowledged gratefully. Not least to Mr William B. Eerdmans, President of William B. Eerdmans Publishing Company, Grand Rapids, Michigan, for encouragement to give renewed consideration to John 13–17, first explored in *The Night He Was Betrayed*, Eerdmans, 1982.

Suggestions for group discussion are provided in the conviction that material so rich is best studied in the cross-lights of shared experience and insight. Above and beyond all else, we seek to understand, to appreciate, and so to enjoy, the profoundest book in the world.

The basis of study is the Revised Standard Version (1946) sometimes compared with second edition (1971) (RSV); with the Greek Testament (United Bible Societies' 3rd edition) (Greek); the New English Bible (NEB); the New International Version (fifth impression) (NIV), and once or twice with the English Revised Version (1881–1885) (RV).

John always means the author of the Gospel; the Baptist is always so called, to avoid confusion. 1 John means the First Epistle of John. Matthew-Mark-Luke signifies the generally similar (or 'synoptic', 'seen together') tradition about Jesus preserved in these three Gospels.

Feeling for the Right Approach

1

What Sort of Book?

We rarely turn to a medical encyclopedia to read something cheerful, or to a legal textbook for something funny. It is well to know what kind of book we are taking up if we are not to be disappointed, or bewildered.

We intend to enjoy John's Gospel, but it was not written to be enjoyed, except in the special sense of enlightenment, enrichment, and strengthening of faith. Yet thousands of Christians have always found it most enjoyable, and it is so still if we approach it in the right way.

John's Gospel is plainly not just another 'life of Jesus'. John begins, not with our Lord's birth, boyhood, baptism, but with the apostolic Church's ultimate assessment of who he was. The only reference to Jesus' birth is delayed to 7:41–52, and mentions Nazareth, not Bethlehem. We are not told Jesus' age, except that he was 'not yet fifty', nor his mother's name. His father is twice called Joseph without qualification. We wait until 7:5 to learn that he had brothers; no number is mentioned, nor any sisters. And he gives five chapters to one evening!

Jesus' kinship with the Baptist is not mentioned; his baptism is not described; his temptation, appointment of the Twelve, crucial enquiry at Caesarea Philippi, transfiguration, Gethsemane agony, and ascension are all omitted. So are all his exorcisms, and healings of lepers. As a retelling of Jesus' story, John's Gospel would be inadequate, and what John does tell he expresses very differently, as we shall see.

John states his purpose

John makes very clear the sort of book he set out to write, the purpose that controls every page and paragraph:

> *Now Jesus did many other signs in the presence of the disciples, which are not written in this book; but these are written that you may believe that Jesus is the Christ, the Son of God, and that believing you may have life in his name.*
>
> John 20:30–31

That says a lot!

It says, first, that John does not tell all he knows, but only a selection.

'Not written in this book' may hint that there were other books, of which John knew, in which further information might be found.

Secondly, John maintains that, though incomplete, his record is accurate. He tells of significant things ('signs') done in the presence of the disciples, whose memories lie behind the record. His stories are no myths, no invented illustrations of great ideas; he tells of things that actually happened, that many witnessed. The Christian faith rests upon historical events.

John says, thirdly, that he has chosen to record things Jesus did which lead us to believe that Jesus is the Christ, the Son of God. He is writing to convince, to argue a point, to make out a case for a far-reaching belief. Namely, that Jesus is the long-expected Messiah of the Jews, and that he stood in so close relation to God that only words like 'Father—Son' could describe it.

John is not conducting an investigation, but persuading us of a truth of which he himself is utterly convinced. His selection of stories has a deliberate theological 'slant'. So John says, and to accept this is to find the right approach to several features of his book that otherwise puzzle us.

It explains the lack of chronological order. Since he is not recounting Christ's story but persuading us who Christ is, John is free to arrange his arguments in any order that suits his purpose. If he places the cleansing of the temple early in his book, while Matthew places it at the end of his, we need not ask who was correct, nor suppose it happened twice: John is not concerned with when it occurred, but with what it foreshadowed.

John's stated purpose explains, too, why he omits events which the other Gospels emphasize, when they do not contribute to his argument. And why at some twenty places he intrudes into the story to draw attention to some fact, or some implications, which we might miss. He does this at length in 3:16–21, 31–36; briefly in 2:24–25 to explain why Jesus did not trust himself to men; in 6:6 to assure us that Jesus did not need Philip's advice; at 7:39 to explain Jesus' words; at 11:51–52 to explain Caiaphas' prophecy, and at numerous other places. So eager is he to carry our minds with him as his argument unfolds.

Nevertheless, John explicitly denies that he is concerned just with ideas and doctrines. His deepest motive in writing, he says, is urgent and practical: 'that you may believe . . . and that believing you may have life in his name' (20:31). John's ultimate motive, after all, is evangelistic. But this statement raises two fundamental questions which must be clarified if we are to understand, and to enjoy, John's message to the full.

'Life' and 'belief' examined

What is this 'life' which John is so eager we should share? Almost his first statement about Jesus declares that 'in him was life'; and 'new birth'—the opportunity to begin life anew—is Jesus' first announcement to Nicodemus. The repeated offer of 'eternal life' to whoever believes shortly follows (3:15–16), to be repeated eight times through the Gospel.

The life so offered certainly includes immortality. Jesus is the resurrection and the life, and whoever believes in Jesus, though he die, yet shall he live (11:25). Christ's sheep 'never perish' (10:28). Because he lives, we shall live also (14:19).

But this eternal life is a present experience. He who hears Christ's word and believes has passed from death to life (5:24). Eternal life is an interior resource, a well-spring within the soul, that refreshes now and issues in immortality hereafter because of its deathless quality (4:14).

That is where John's emphasis falls, on the nature of the life seen at its highest in Jesus as the very light of men (1:4), and given to whomsoever Jesus wills (5:21). It is an 'abundant', overflowing life, nourished by Christ's own flesh and blood, enriched by his words that are 'spirit and life' (6:54, 63), and continually enlightened (8:12).

Jesus is himself the life (as he is also the way and the truth) for each believer; so the ground and essence of this living experience is to know God and Jesus whom he sent (17:3). Such is the life of eternal quality, incomparable, inexhaustible, immortal, which John longs to share with all who read and will believe.

What, then, is this 'believing' which John represents as the sole condition of eternal life? John says that when Jews asked Jesus, 'What must we do, to be doing the works of God?' Jesus himself replied, 'This is the work of God, that you believe in him whom he has sent' (6:28–29). And John uses the word ninety-six times to describe the only adequate response to Jesus' coming.

It is significant that John never speaks of 'faith', which might be understood as a settled, static 'frame of mind', but always of 'believing'—an active, living, responsive outreach of mind and soul, sometimes towards Jesus' works or his word; sometimes towards facts or statements concerning him ('believe that I am he'; 'believe this'). Occasionally John sums up acceptance of who Jesus is as 'belief in his name', 'receiving' him; more often of believing in a general way—'that all might believe'—suggesting passage from sceptical resistance to acceptance, openness to God and to truth. Most often John speaks of 'believing in' the Father, the Son, the truth, implying trust and conviction; or of 'coming to' Jesus, that is, turning to him in need, which expresses neatly how 'believing' includes entrusting oneself to Jesus.

And so do John's seven references to 'following' Jesus as a leader implicitly believed in. And his twelve references to 'loving' Jesus, which carries belief to the point of total adherence of mind and heart to all that Jesus is and stands for. Such trusting, accepting loyalty, sustained against temptation and adversity, is 'abiding' in Jesus (ten references).

Believers are called 'disciples' (forty-eight times), suggesting the pupil status of those who by progressive believing come to 'know' Jesus, the Father, the teaching—the thought is expressed twenty times. John makes much of the gift of knowledge and spiritual insight which believing in Jesus confers. By means of it, those who otherwise merely 'see' events superficially come to 'perceive' their deeper meaning (9:39–41).

It is to this 'believing'—which grows with deepening trust into sure knowledge, and confers eternal life—that John, as he writes, strives to bring us. The result is a book which even yet is a favourite and powerful tool of evangelism. Yet it is also greatly treasured by the maturest of believers. John's Gospel is essentially evangelistic—and also an inexhaustible textbook for masterclass Christians! It seems that this odd ambivalence was noted by some very early copyists.

An instructive ambiguity

For in the oldest manuscripts of 20:31 a single letter, inserted or omitted by Christian scribes, leaves it uncertain whether John wrote 'these things are written that you might come to believe', or 'that you might continue to believe'. Is John seeking to create belief where none exists, or to confirm it in face of persecution, doubt, or false teaching?

The evidence of the manuscripts is so evenly balanced that the United Bible Society's Greek Testament (3rd Edition) actually prints the doubtful word both ways at once. If we review what John has written to discover which audience he has in mind—unbelievers, or troubled believers—we meet the same uncertainty.

For John delights to parade examples of people coming to believe in Jesus: Andrew, Peter, Philip, Nathanael, Nicodemus (eventually), the woman of Samaria, her fellow-citizens, a nobleman at Cana, a paralytic at Bethzatha, 'many people' in Jerusalem, a blind man at Siloam's pool, the Bethany sisters, 'many even of the authorities', Thomas. 'Look at them', says John, 'all finding their way to belief: Look—and believe!' The example and contagion of others' experience is part of John's strategy in winning new believers.

But equally clearly, John shows that such belief in Jesus is no once-for-all-time, settled-in-a-moment event: belief must grow, deepen, struggle against set-backs, temptations, doubt, until it reaches certainty. We read of some, already disciples, who at later points 'believed', at Cana, in the Upper Room, at the empty tomb (2:11; 16:29–30; 20:8–9). We are jolted, sometimes, by the disciples' incomprehension. They are surprised to find Jesus talking with a woman, and at his having found 'something to eat'. They are bewildered about what to do with enquiring Greeks. They are puzzled at some of Jesus' sayings (16:17–18), and his deeds (13:6–8).

We are told repeatedly that the disciples did not understand until long afterwards (2:22; 12:16; 20:9), and had much to learn as late as the eve of the crucifixion (13:7; 14:20, 26; 16:12–13; compare 1:50). They betray a tendency to argue with Jesus, as not yet in awe of him (11:7–16; 13:36–14:5; 16:16–18). Aware of this Jesus asks (as though examining their faith) 'Do you believe?', 'Have I been with you so long and yet you do not know me...?'

In the last conversation before his death Jesus explicitly asks for their belief (14:1, 11), and hints that they cannot yet believe as they will do later (14:29; 16:23, 25). Slow progress in believing was especially true of Thomas, the late developer among disciples.

Nor did Jesus assume that all who began to believe would grow to conviction: 'If you continue in my word, you are truly my disciples...' (8:31). He had witnessed the 'drawing back' of many (6:66). Hence his exhortation that the Eleven would 'abide in the vine', and his prayer that the Father would 'keep' them in the years to come. There is nothing automatic about growth in faith.

As we shall see, John often assumes that his readers have some knowledge of Jesus' story. This tends to confirm that he has immature or sorely-tried believers also before his mind. The truth is that the book serves unbelievers, enquirers and hard-pressed believers equally well. John's purpose is clear: to promote belief in Jesus as Messiah and Son of God, so as to share the eternal life which Jesus offers with as many as possible, whatever stage they have reached in the journey of faith.

2

The Book Itself

John's Gospel makes a very thin paperback, about fifty-two pages, but it usually comes bound together with sixty-five other religious books, or with twenty-six other Christian books, among these three 'lives' of Jesus. Thus a special context is given to the book, and certain comparisons become inevitable. We cannot study it in complete isolation.

It is an ancient book, from the first Christian century, almost certainly written originally in Greek. When the precise meaning of any passage is discussed, accurate translation rests upon dictionary evidence of the meaning of Greek words, not upon tradition, or personal preference for what 'sounds nicer'.

Again, for all its apparent simplicity, John's Gospel is certainly one of the profoundest books in the world. For all these reasons, it is well to consider the book as a whole, and its background, before examining its various parts, if we are to appreciate it properly and enjoy it as we should.

What does it say?

The habit of reading Scripture in short sections is especially misleading in the case of a book so closely argued as this Gospel. An overview of the contents reveals an almost architectural unity of structure which no snatches chosen here and there can possibly reflect. The late division into chapters and verses takes no account of this underlying pattern, and is best ignored. But that pattern must be discovered, not invented and imposed upon the book; to discover it, we note carefully exactly what the author says, and what he emphasizes.

John refers seventeen times to the 'signs' Jesus performed, uses a related word another three times, and speaks of his 'works' (with almost the same meaning) a further nine times. Of these twenty-nine references to the same thought, at least twelve link it with belief in Jesus. Such insistence must provide some clue to John's main theme.

John begins to count Jesus' signs, though in the end they prove to be too many (2:11; 4:54; 20:30). These signs distinguish Christ's ministry from that of the Baptist (10:41), and because of them crowds gathered to Jesus, repeatedly testifying to the impression the signs made. The

Jewish authorities also so testified, and frequently demanded more. Jesus rebuked this demand (4:48), and John remarks that, although many believed when they saw the signs, 'Jesus did not trust himself to them' (2:24). John adds that despite so many signs, the popular Jewish attitude remained sceptical.

The crowds were willing enough to gape at wonders and benefit from miracles, but they refused to perceive the truth about Jesus which the 'signs' signified, and demanded more proof (6:30).

Jesus' signs were also 'works' appointed by the Father for the Son to accomplish. No one else had done such works; they are indeed 'the works of the Father' who dwells in Christ and 'does his works'. Because they are God-like deeds, they bear testimony that Jesus has been sent by the Father. They constitute the Father's witness to Jesus (5:36; 10:25; 15:24). If the Jews, or the disciples, cannot believe Christ's words, let them 'believe the works... believe me for the sake of the works themselves' (10:37–38; 14:11–12).

But always it is the quality of Jesus' works, as no mere wonders but good, health-giving, compassionate, life-enhancing, Father-like, which bears witness to their divine origin. So, to 'believe the works' is rightly to read their meaning, to discern that he who feeds the five thousand is the bread of life; that he who raised Lazarus is indeed the resurrection and the life. To see miracles saves no one: to see and believe the meaning of the miracles is to accept that Jesus has been sent by God with divine authority and power.

This constant emphasis upon 'signs' and 'works' cannot be accidental. In these, John insists, Jesus 'manifested his glory', so kindling belief (2:11). This is the predominant and persistent theme of John. Throughout he is telling how Jesus manifested his glory. On the Gospel's first page John bears his own testimony, speaking for the whole Church, 'We have beheld his glory, glory as of the only Son from the Father', and repeats the gospel's invitation to all, 'Come and see'. This is John's good news: the divine Son has been steadily unveiled, 'made known', among men.

The Baptist says he came to initiate this revealing of Jesus (1:31, 34). Cana sees Jesus manifesting his glory; Jesus' brothers urge him to 'show himself to the world', though it was not yet Jesus' purpose to go up to Jerusalem 'manifestly' (7:10 Greek). Jesus speaks of the works of God being 'made manifest'. In the Upper Room, Jesus promises to reveal himself still further (14:21), and in his prayer declares that he has 'manifested' God's name to the men God has given him. To Caiaphas, Jesus claims always to have spoken 'revealingly' (Greek); after the resurrection Jesus is still 'manifesting' himself (21:1, 14); commenting on Jesus' whole ministry, John asks Isaiah's question: 'To whom has the arm of the Lord been revealed?'

From this reiteration of 'signs' performed, 'works' with divine meanings, and progressive self-manifestation, it is clear that John thinks of the life and ministry of Jesus as a gradual unveiling of something long promised but hitherto hidden—the glory of the Son of God incarnate among men. He intends to recount the successive steps in that self-manifestation of the divine Son, in order that we too shall see his glory, shall believe in him, and so share the life he offers.

A tentative outline

As we look more closely at what John has written we perceive changes of emphasis within that overmastering theme. In chapters 2–4 Jesus begins to make himself known by striking deeds and stimulating conversations about the temple, the Law, the Baptist's prophesying, and worship. In all, a clear contrast may be discerned between what Jesus offers and the best that Judaism can give.

In chapters 5–12, the placid tone changes to one of prolonged argument and conflict of ideas, provoked mainly by Jesus' claims to be the fulfilment of Judaism, of its festivals and its faith. He is God's representative, the giver of true manna, the water and the light of life, the sole shepherd of God's fold, the giver of immortality.

Each claim is hotly disputed, and the conflict ends with an official decision to kill Jesus. After each controversy, Jesus 'withdrew', 'hid himself', 'went away across the Jordan', 'went into the country near the wilderness', 'departed and hid himself from them' (5:13; 6:15; 8:59; 10:40; 11:54; 12:36). So Jesus evades repeated attempts to stone or to arrest him, each failing 'because his hour was not yet come'. Then, at the end, 'The hour has come . . .', 'For this purpose I have come to this hour' (12:23, 27; 13:1; 17:1; nine references in all).

When Jesus withdraws from public ministry for the last time, John comments that the Jews' rejection only fulfils Isaiah's prophecy concerning God's 'despised and rejected' servant.

Chapters 13–17 tell therefore of Jesus' continued self-manifestation to his own inner circle in the Upper Room as the servant who cleanses the people of God. The approaching cross, the resurrection, the coming of the Spirit, all prepare for a final revelation of Christ's glory. In his parting prayer, Jesus asks for that consummation of his work—'glorify thou me . . .' (17:5)—and that God will guard and keep united the men he leaves to continue his mission.

Chapters 18–20 are more purely narrative, though even here John is concerned to show Jesus revealed as the wholly innocent lamb of God, sacrificed at Passover to take away the sin of the world, but rising again to ascend to the Father and bestow the Spirit. This, too, is an unveiling of Christ's glory, for John repeatedly uses the term 'glorified' to describe the total act of death-resurrection-ascension which Jesus accomplished by his passion (7:39; 12:16, 23, 27–31; 13:31–33; 17:1; compare a parallel use of the word at 21:19).

The climax of John's whole argument is reached in a hesitant disciple's confession of Jesus as 'My Lord and my God'. There John's brief statement of intent closes the main work.

These four 'stages' of Jesus' self-manifestation are prefaced by a series of testimonies borne to Jesus by the evangelist, the Baptist, and the first disciples. They are closed with a chapter of 'afterthoughts', a postscript recording Peter's restoration after his denial of Christ, and explaining a current misunderstanding concerning the beloved disciple. Anonymous friends then briefly commend John's book to all readers.

Such an overview of John's Gospel yields the tentative outline presented on our contents page—'tentative' because it must be checked, assessed and altered, as we read; otherwise it will get in our way, and John's.

An accompanying note?

No two biblical books are so alike as the Gospel of John and the brief gem of an epistle we call 'First John'. Of the epistle's 295 different words 226 are found in the Gospel, together with fifty phrases, numerous key-words, familiar contrasts, several features of Greek style, and a common theological outlook. The opening lines of Gospel and epistle are closely similar; the main theme, a true assessment of Jesus as divine Son incarnate, is the same in both.

This theme is argued in the epistle against certain divisive Greek ideas. We miss therefore the anti-Judaist controversy of the Gospel and the appeal to the Old Testament. In all else, the Gospel and the epistle are plainly from the same background, the same Christian tradition, the same 'school' of evangelism.

Whether they are from the same pen, or from a master and his 'disciple'; whether the note accompanied or followed the Gospel, applying its message to a local situation; or the appeal for true faith and unity was sent first and the Gospel written later to reinforce it; whether we can only understand certain things in the epistle if we refer back to the Gospel—all are questions debated for a long time, and still unsettled.

Neither book may be allowed to 'control' the interpretation of the other, for no writer needs to repeat himself precisely. But it is sometimes useful to note how certain words, expressions, thoughts, are used in 1 John when we are debating what they mean in the Gospel. At least we can fairly say, from noticing 1 John, that such and such a meaning, or idea, was current 'in the Johannine circle' in New Testament times.

3

For Whom Did John Write?

Each Gospel-writer wrote for his contemporary Church and its adherents, addressing a current situation. To know the people and the circumstances addressed often illumines the meaning. Moreover, every earnest evangelist must address his audience in their own terms if he wishes to be understood. So from the themes John emphasizes, the terms he uses, his way of putting things, we may endeavour to picture the readers he had in mind.

For Jews? For Greeks? For Samaritans?

To appreciate John's Gospel fully requires a fair knowledge of Judaism. We are expected to know its sabbath rules, to recognize some twenty Old Testament quotations, to be familiar with Jewish temple worship, the great festivals, the Law, rabbinic authority, and the powers of the Jewish Sanhedrin under Roman overlordship. Abraham, Jacob, Moses, Elijah, the Messiah, the latest Jewish prophet (the Baptist), all come before us without introduction.

John does not explain God's creating by a spoken word, nor the serpent on a pole, the manna in the wilderness, the prophet promised by Moses, the law of purification, the Jewish attitude to Samaritans, the title 'Son of man'. The list of Jewish ideas John assumes his readers to understand is long—for example, the good shepherd of God's fold, Israel as the vine God planted in the earth, the history behind the Passover, and the feast of Tabernacles, Micah's prophecy concerning Bethlehem (7:42), the expectation that Messiah would live for ever.

Nevertheless, John's attitude to Jewish affairs is curiously ambivalent. He argues that Jesus fulfils every Jewish insight and hope, as the true Word of God to the world, the true shepherd, pillar of fire, manna, and light of the world, the one long prophesied as king, the real lamb of God and sacrifice for sin, the genuine servant of the Lord, older than Abraham. So Jesus set a glowing seal of approval upon Jewish thought and expectations. 'Salvation is from the Jews' (4:22); and after all, Jesus was a Jew.

For all that, throughout this Gospel the leaders of opposition to Jesus are 'the Jews'. The differences between Sadducees, Pharisees, scribes, and 'common people', so familiar in the other Gospels, are here largely ignored. By John's time they no longer mattered, and Jewish opposition to Christianity had hardened into a nationalist stance.

John emphasizes constantly that 'the Jews' did not recognize Jesus, and became his bitterest enemies. 'He came to his own home, and his own people received him not.' Caiaphas the High Priest and the Jewish supreme court, bear in John's eyes the heaviest guilt of Jesus' rejection and death.

And John shows that this enmity, arising from similar causes, persisted into his own later time. Each of the evangelists handles the story in this way, telling of the past in ways relevant to their own present. We can trace in later Jewish literature the charges against Jesus that John describes, as still repeated against the Church.

That Jesus came from Nazareth, not from David's Bethlehem as prophets foretold; that he ministered as an ignorant layman in remote, 'provincial' Galilee; that the Jewish leaders of the time, with full evidence before them, saw through his claims; that Pilate, with the full authority of Roman justice, condemned Jesus as a common felon: all was still being said when John wrote. Above all, that Jesus (and the Church) talked horrifying nonsense about eating his flesh and drinking his blood; and committed blasphemy in making Jesus 'equal with God'.

Patiently, point by point, John replies with force to precisely these cavils, setting each Christian claim in its true light, and exposing the real motive behind Jewish rejection. Thus there can be no doubt, from what John contends as clearly as from what he assumes, that he is addressing Jewish readers. For that reason it is necessary occasionally to refer to contemporary Jewish writers like Philo (about 20BC to AD50), Josephus (AD37–100), rabbinic commentators, and to collections of Jewish laws and debates like the Talmud and the Mishnah (from the early Christian centuries but preserving older sources).

But did John address Jews only? From John's opening paragraph almost to the end we are aware of an atmosphere of deep reflection, prolonged theological debate, something approaching philosophical mysticism, quite unlike anything in the Old Testament, in Matthew's Gospel, or even in Paul.

The eternal 'Logos' (Word, reason), the agent in creation and source of the 'light' of human reason and conscience, is a typically Greek idea, although it has distant parallels in Jewish thought. The emphasis on divine sonship, on immortality, on Jesus' complete self-sufficiency (asking for no information, in charge of every situation, manipulating events, suffering neither temptation nor agony), is all congenial to the Greek mind.

So too are John's repeated contrasts, life and death, light and darkness, truth and falsehood, love and hatred, flesh and spirit, God and the world, not unlike Greek dualism. The idea of life as marked out beforehand by a pattern of crucial 'hours' somewhat resembles the Greek conception of individual 'fate'.

Most of all would John's emphasis upon knowledge attract Greek readers. 'This is eternal life, that they know...'; 'O righteous Father, the world has not known thee, but I have known thee; and these know that thou hast sent me...' 'To know' and its derivatives occur in John's 876 verses at least 118 times (once for every seven-and-a-half verses); quite often even its commonplace occurrences have overtones of deeper meaning (8:19 and 14:9 for examples).

Men reject the truth because they do not know God, Jesus says; the disciples do know him, and shall know more. Even the Jews, despite centuries of revelation, do not know God as Jesus knows him (8:54–55). Greek readers would find such arguments persuasive. In another way, it is significant that, according to John, Jesus' public ministry to Jews ceased with the arrival of 'certain Greeks'.

This does not mean that John turned to pagan sources for his message, or that he borrowed his ideas of baptism, sacred meals, and eternal life, from the widespread mystery religions. It shows only that he knew his contemporaries, sought to communicate with them in terms they understood, and to emphasize those themes in Jesus' teaching which they would find attractive. It has been shown that of John's twelve leading topics (the Logos, light, life, rebirth, etc.) eleven have their seed-thoughts in the other Gospels, eleven are also foreshadowed in Jewish teaching, and all twelve have parallels in pagan—mainly Greek—thought.

It seems probable that John knew something of that strange mixture of beliefs, fears, philosophy, superstitions and obscenities that came to be known from its emphasis upon knowledge, as 'Gnosticism' (Greek *gnosis* = knowledge). To Gnostics, everything material was inherently, incurably, evil; only mind and spirit were redeemable, and capable of immortality. Salvation, immortality, depended wholly upon knowledge of certain spiritual truths. Morality was irrelevant, and Gnosticism was 'loveless to the core'.

Matter being evil, God could not have created it, or become incarnate, or suffer; incarnation, atonement, resurrection, were all mere appearances only. A chain of beings, of ascending spirituality, mediated between man and the infinitely distant God. To know these things was alone necessary to salvation.

By the second century, Gnosticism was everywhere condemned by the Church, but at first some Christians found it attractive as an 'advanced' stage of Christian understanding. 1 John was written to combat its influence in the churches, and much in John's Gospel is equally appropriate as a reply to Gnostic teaching. Yet one ancient copy contains an introduction claiming that the Gospel was written by a Gnostic teacher, and the oldest of existing commentaries on it is by a Gnostic!

In truth, of course, John's constant insistence that 'the Word became flesh', and hungered, wearied, thirsted, bled and died; that God loved the world, and Jesus commanded us to love; that sin blinds and alienates the soul and needs to be forgiven—all is anti-Gnostic, however John's language might (perhaps purposely) attract Gnostics' attention.

That John should address himself to Jewish and to Greek minds at the same time seems improbable, until we remember that Greeks had ruled Palestine for over a century. Their influence lingered through names like Andrew, Philip, Stephen (see Acts 6:5 also); through 'Hellenists' (Jews of Greek education and sympathies, see Acts 6:1–6; 9:29; 11:20 and margin); and through some early Gnostic groups among Jews, traces of which many be found in Galatians, Colossians, Jude, 2 Peter and Revelation. The Decapolis was in Jesus' time a region east and south-east of Galilee, Greek in population and constitution. Ethnic distinctions were not so rigid in Palestine as we might suppose; Pilate wrote his inscription above Jesus' cross in three familiar languages—including Greek.

John may have been aware, too, of the non-conforming Jewish sect living in monastic retreat some twenty-five miles from where the Baptist ministered, near the Dead Sea. These held themselves aloof from the temple and the hierarchy, claiming to be the true Israel of the divine covenant. For parallels to John's language and insights we need not travel further than Qumran.

Also on the fringe of Judaism were the unorthodox Samaritans, claiming descent from Jacob (4:12), holding to the books of Moses only, to their own priesthood and synagogues, cherishing sites and shrines sacred to Israel long before the settlement in Canaan. Samaria had proved fruitful ground for early Christian evangelism (Acts 1:8; 8:4–25), and John traces this back to the visit of Jesus himself, giving the full story (4:1–42). John records also the charge that Jesus was a Samaritan heretic (8:48), and lets it pass unanswered.

Amid all these influences in the thought-world which John addressed, his own thinking remained firmly under the control of his transforming experience of Christ. He borrows only the terms and contrasts with which to illustrate the superiority of the gospel. The result is a wonderfully rich and powerful statement of the Christian message to the world intellectually confused, morally at a loss, and deeply hungry for new truth, a better hope, and a nearer God.

For the world and the future?

Matthew, Mark and Luke show Jesus ministering mainly against the background of orthodox Judaism, its scribes, priests, Pharisees, Sadducees, synagogue worship and festivals. When Jerusalem was destroyed by Rome (AD67–70), the temple disappeared, the priesthood was scattered, and all Jews were banished from Judea. Orthodox Judaism, the matrix of Christianity, became impossible to maintain.

The future did not lie with animal sacrifice, racial election, Old Testament Law, circumcision, and scrupulous bondage to the past. John, in effect, liberated Christianity from its original Judaist limitations. He retained its firm foundation in historic events in Palestine, but he preached Christian truth in Gentile terms to the wider world of Greek philosophy, Roman discipline, polytheistic religion, and a myriad mystical cults. (Philo, the Jewish propagandist, had similarly sought to build a bridge between the Jewish and pagan worlds by re-presenting Old Testament stories as illustrations of Greek thinking).

John thus completed Paul's work, transforming Christianity from a sect within Judaism (like those of the Pharisees and Sadducees, see Acts 5:17; 15:5; 24:5, 14; 28:22; the Greek word is the same throughout—'sect'), into a world religion, and sent it on its way through history to benefit all nations.

It has been suggested that in the catastrophic destruction of the Jewish State, Christianity might well have evaporated as a philosophy, or petrified into an outworn ritual. That it persisted and grew as a living faith, grounded in history but renewed in each generation, and adapted to many cultures, is due under God mainly to Paul's world missions, and John's transplanting the gospel into new soil before its Judaist roots had entirely withered, and re-minting Jewish-Christian thought into the intellectual coinage of the wider world and the future.

For us, too?

That John wrote for a specific time and audience does not at all imply that the Spirit was not prompting him to write also for all times, people, and circumstances. The right approach to all Scripture is first to ask what God was saying through the author at that time to the people to whom it was sent, concerning their situation. It is not for us to make what we like of what God said. But the second question is no less important: how far does our need and situation so resemble theirs that the message given to them homes in upon our hearts as the voice of God speaking still?

It scarcely needs saying that John's account of Jesus does just that. For the source of the book is not really John but Jesus: that gives persistence, timelessness, penetration and power to everything John says. History justifies such claims; for the book is treasured and loved in every part of the modern world, after some eighteen centuries. To argue such a claim is like arguing the beauty of a rose, the truth of an axiom, the value of kindness. One can only repeat John's invitation, quoting Jesus, 'Come and see!'—and let the book do its own work in receptive minds and hearts.

But 'eighteen' centuries? Yes, because the book found slow acceptance, and its preservation was at some cost. There are reasons (but no proofs) for thinking that John's Gospel originated in either Antioch or Ephesus. The earliest fragment we possess came from Egypt, probably from the first half of the second century. Allowing time for copies to reach Egypt, recent expert opinion suggests AD70–90 for the Gospel's date. The argument in 9:22, 34; 10:7–9 about who has the right to exclude anyone from God's fold, would be especially relevant around AD85, when Christian Jews were formally excluded from the synagogues. It would have been pointless long afterwards.

Yet mid-second-century Christian writers, referring to John and familiar with Ephesus, do not mention John's Gospel. A Gnostic teacher cited it about AD135. One Christian group actually rejected John's Gospel. The revered Justin Martyr (died AD165) sounds doubtful about its authority. It was used in a symposium of the Gospels about AD170, but by a Christian of doubtful orthodoxy. A list of books approved for use in Christian worship at Rome, issued AD180–200, includes John's Gospel while still labouring at length to defend it. Thereafter the Gospel became widely accepted as Christian Scripture.

It seems strange that the Church took so long to accept such a book. We must remember the conditions of the time, and keep them in mind as we read. Christian communities were widely scattered; communications were slow; the only copies available were handwritten and extremely expensive.

Papyrus rolls were brittle and short-lived; we know that fragments were frequently lost, and whole portions misplaced. The original copy of John's Gospel has long since perished, and no statements about what it contained have any ground at all. We possess only copies, recopied, and again recopied, by hand, over a thousand years. Copyists were professionally trained and careful, but not infallible—hence the footnotes in modern versions drawing attention to variations in the text according to 'ancient authorities' (or 'witnesses', or 'manuscripts').

Despite these difficult conditions, and the Church's long neglect, John's Gospel was preserved for the enlightenment and blessing of countless generations of Christians. God's way is ever that of incarnation, the divine mediated through the human, the timeless through the temporary, eternal truth through occasional and fallible means. That the divine, the timeless, the eternally true, does in fact come to us through John's immense achievement, no earnest heart can doubt.

4

What Has John Done With Jesus' Story?

That John's account of Jesus is very different from that of the other Gospels is obvious from the numerous 'omissions' which show that he is not simply rewriting the life of Jesus. We noted, too, the quite distinctive theological tone of John's account. In addition, much of what John does share with Matthew-Mark-Luke is differently arranged—the cleansing of the temple; the ministry mainly in Jerusalem at several festivals (Mark has only one, but note 'how often...' in Luke 13:34); the call of disciples; the ride into Jerusalem; the last meal with the Twelve; the visits to the empty tomb.

Even more striking is the material John alone preserves—the miracle at Cana; the visit of Nicodemus; the conversation in Samaria; the cure of the paralytic; the quick-witted blind man; the raising of Lazarus; the coming of the Greeks; the washing of the disciples' feet; the Upper Room conversation and prayer; the promises concerning the Spirit; the interview in the garden; the convincing of Thomas; the restoration of Peter. One wonders how the other evangelists could tell the story, omitting these precious elements.

A different story?

For these contributions by John to our knowledge of Jesus we must be deeply grateful, while acknowledging that had we only John, we would have sorely missed the matchless parables, the sermon on the mount, the Lord's Prayer, the institution of the eucharist, the memorable poetic lines, sharp epigrams, provoking paradoxes, and vivid metaphors describing life in God's kingdom. We would miss, too, the birthstories, the boyhood, the temptation and the Jesus of the hillsides and seashore, the synagogues and the houses of the common people, among the sick and surrounded by children.

In John's Gospel, Jesus is more often among religious leaders in the city, debating the nature of God, his own person, the means of revelation, the sources of authority, immortality. Jesus certainly sounds different, in John's account, sometimes repetitious and argumentative, just occasionally mystifying.

Much may be due to differences of selection and emphasis; but there are also differences of fact which cannot be overlooked. It is difficult now to decide whether Jesus began his ministry in Galilee only after the Baptist was imprisoned (Mark 1:14), or alongside the Baptist at the Jordan (John 3:22–24); whether during Jesus' lifetime the Baptist was recognized as the promised Elijah (Matthew 17:10–13) or himself stoutly denied it (John 1:21); whether Simon of Cyrene carried Christ's cross part way to Calvary (Mark 15:21) or Jesus 'carried his own' (John 19:17).

In Matthew-Mark-Luke the great turning points of Jesus' career are his baptism and temptation, the confession of his messiahship at Caesarea Philippi, his entry to Jerusalem, and his cleansing of the temple. According to John, they were the marriage at Cana where he manifested his glory; the feeding of the five thousand where the crowd attempted to crown him king; his provocative claims at the feast of Tabernacles; and the raising of Lazarus, which according to John sealed his fate.

Mark insists that Jesus did not publicly claim, or accept from others, any messianic title, until he was ready to challenge Jerusalem and die (Mark 1:25, 34; 3:11–12; 8:29–30; 9:9; 10:46—11:10). This was important: the title was politically dangerous, popularly misleading. John appears to ignore this necessary caution, though out of some fifteen references to Jesus' messiahship, four are quite private, in another four the crowd discuss the possibility, and in a further four Pilate and the soldiers deride the suggestion, neither situation requiring comment from Jesus. Direct challenge on the question is met by evasion (10:24–26; 12:34–36; 18:32–34). The title 'Son of Man' was too ambiguous to cause trouble.

John's account of Jesus' attitude to the dangerous title does not therefore directly contradict Mark's. But John does not emphasize nearly so much the caution of Jesus on this point. Of course, neither the claim itself, nor Jesus' public attitude to it, was any longer dangerous by the time John wrote.

One major divergence of John's story from that of the earlier Gospels concerns the evening upon which Jesus ate his farewell meal with the disciples. Matthew and Luke, following Mark, say that this was the Passover meal and Jesus died the next day (Matthew 26:17–19; Mark 14:12–16; Luke 22:7–13). John says the meal took place on the day before the Passover, and that Jesus died with the Passover lambs (13:1, 29; 18:28; 19:14, 31, 36, 42; note 1 Corinthians 5:7). The Passover lamb, slain within the temple was not available on the eve of Passover. Jesus certainly died on Friday, eve-of-sabbath (Mark 15:42; John 19:31);

28

but was that Friday Passover Day (John) or the day following Passover (Matthew-Mark-Luke)?

After a century's learned discussion, and innumerable attempted explanations and compromises, this divergence in the accounts remains unresolved. Was John relying upon a different tradition, deliberately correcting the earlier version, or simply underlining the truth that Jesus was 'the lamb of God that bears away the sin of the world'—a truth more important to him than mere accuracy of dates?

Not another Jesus!

Whatever the differences of presentation between John's Gospel and the earlier ones, in their portraits of Jesus himself they overlap far more than they diverge. Not only do main events recur in all, but innumerable details of place, time, personality, thought and background. Sayings like 'destroy this temple', 'a prophet is not without honour...', 'a servant is not greater than his lord', 'he that loves (or hates) his life', 'Be of good cheer'; and ideas like the faithful shepherd, God's vineyard (or vine); a significant confession by Peter, an anointing of Christ's feet, a significant healing of blindness, God as Father, and Jesus as prophet, servant, and Lord, and many more, are all common to the four Gospels.

John records two 'beatitudes' which the other Gospels omit (13:17; 20:29). Matthew (11:25) and Luke (10:21) preserve a saying by Jesus—'All things have been delivered to me by my Father, and no one knows the Son except the Father, and no one knows the Father except the Son and any one to whom the Son chooses to reveal him. Come to me...'—which has the very accent of John's record.

Some fifty examples have been found of turns of phrase character-istic of Jesus in Matthew-Mark-Luke which resemble those in John's story, sometimes disguised in translation from Jesus' Aramaic into Greek. (No 'authorized' translation of Jesus' sayings existed until the Gospels became familiar.) The pithy and often startling utterances we expect in Matthew-Mark-Luke have their parallels in John's record—'He that receives you receives me...', 'Blessed are those who have not seen and yet believe', 'My kingdom is not of this world', 'He who loves his life loses it', 'Night comes when no man can work', 'The truth shall make you free'; and for phrases that shock—'He who eats my flesh and drinks my blood...', 'Before Abraham was I am', 'You are of your father the devil'.

As with the style of speech, so with the form of argument, the representation of Jesus agrees in both records. Jesus appeals from contemporary Jewish teaching to the original divine revelation, in Matthew-Mark-Luke concerning marriage, divorce, the sabbath, the

Law; in John's account concerning the manna in the wilderness, the promise of Abraham, God's resting on the sabbath, the deceitfulness of the devil, and his murderous character. In both records, Jesus argues from what the Father is seen doing—'He makes his sun rise on the evil and the good . . .', 'Your heavenly Father feeds them . . .' and 'My Father is working still . . .'. In all the Gospels, debate frequently proceeds from a 'deep saying' or parable misunderstood, repeated somewhat differently, and so explained. The portraits are consistent, the same mind is at work.

An exceptionally well-qualified Jewish scholar has contended that Jesus' teaching style, according to John's report, is very close indeed to that of learned rabbinic discussions of similar date. As to substance, the arguments in John's account about Jesus' person and origin are not all that different from arguments in Matthew-Mark-Luke about Jesus' claim to forgive sins, to heal on the sabbath, to be Lord of nature and of demons. In the earlier Gospels many prophets and righteous men longed to see Christ's day, and to reject him is blasphemy; in John's Gospel, Abraham rejoiced to see Christ's day, and not to believe in Jesus is to incur judgment.

John adds greatly to our knowledge of Jesus' teaching about the Spirit, but says nothing essentially different from Luke's record. Enough has been said to justify the conclusion that though John has gone about his work in his own way, and has produced a largely 'original' account of the Church's teaching about Jesus, yet it is not so 'totally different' as some have contended. He is certainly telling of the same ministry of the same Jesus as fills the pages of Matthew-Mark-Luke. And once her initial hesitation had passed, the Church has found no difficulty in accepting all four Gospels as authentic and consistent—or in thanking God for their diversity.

What then has John done?

All four Gospels preserve the accumulated testimonies and treasured memories of Jesus' contemporaries, told by parents to children, by disciples to converts, told and retold in every gathering of Christians for worship and counsel. For some two generations all was repeated orally, until the passing of the eye-witnesses prompted requests for written records of their teaching. By about AD85, when Luke was completed, 'many have undertaken to compile a narrative of the things which have been accomplished . . . as they were delivered . . . by those who from the beginning were eyewitnesses' (Luke 1:1–4).

Each chose from the common tradition about Jesus what would best suit his immediate pastoral or evangelistic purpose. It is uncertain whether John knew the earlier Gospels, but he knew the oral traditions upon which they drew, and often reveals his knowledge of things he did not choose to describe but which he expects his readers to know. He does not record Christ's agony in Gethsemane, yet he refers clearly to Christ's prayer on that occasion (12:27; 18:11). He alludes briefly, without explanation, to the Lord's 'supper' (13:4), to Christ's baptism (1:32), to the disciple band, to Jesus' mother, to Mary and Martha, to Nazareth, to Pilate's involvement in Christ's death, to 'many other signs which Jesus did', and much else, always assuming we shall understand.

Yet John did not write to correct, to supplement, or to supersede the other Gospels. He used the traditions about Jesus which they used, selecting and arranging for his own purpose—to demonstrate the divine sonship of Jesus in order that others may share eternal life. His ordering of his materials is logically, not chronologically, planned. And he abbreviates narrative (except in chapter 9) in order to dwell upon meaning. He writes always with the retrospect of long reflection upon a faith enlightened and matured by experience (2:22; 12:16; note 14:26; 16:12). It is this deliberate proportion between incident and reflective discussion that lends to the Gospel its more theological tone.

Other notes of the passage of time are: the way John confronts (as we saw) the later criticisms of Jews against Christianity; the assumption that Gentiles are now within the fold of God, without argument; the need to answer the sect that continued for decades to extol the Baptist above Jesus; and John's caution about over-stressing the sacramental actions without truly sacramental experience (he does not describe Christ's baptism or his command to baptize, nor the supper and the command to celebrate it, yet he dwells upon the meaning of both).

That such hindsight has mingled with memory in John's writing is repeatedly admitted (2:22; 7:39; 12:16; 21:19, 22–23; see 1:14). It is clear in his story of the feeding of the five thousand, with its eucharistic conclusion, and in the strange passage about water and blood flowing from Christ's side. John is looking back to Jesus, certainly, but looking back a long way, and writing for his own contemporaries.

As a result, with Matthew-Mark-Luke on one side and John's Gospel on the other, we have two eyes with which to watch Jesus. John's portrait of him is lifelike, powerful, invaluable. Its chief impression is of One whom no one book or portrait or personal testimony could adequately describe; One who, being divine, voluntarily came among humankind to reveal God, to teach truth, to impart the Spirit, to cleanse humanity by bearing its sin, and to bestow immortality.

In fact, John's portrait of Jesus is quite priceless—and truly astonishing.

5

Jesus Through John's Eyes

The special light which John throws upon the figure of Jesus is more than an effect of selection and emphasis. Here, the retrospect of faith enlightened by experience mounts to an inspired insight into the profoundest theological truth. The Jesus of hillside and shore, at home along life's common ways, is transfigured with a divine radiance that anticipates glory.

Jesus is still 'Rabbi' (eight times), 'prophet' (six times), no divine apparition, or God in disguise, but indisputably a real man, the Word made flesh. He grew weary, slept, was thirsty and hungry, was troubled (five times), wept real tears, bled and bore wounds, was moved with 'zeal', saddened by desertion, perhaps even hesitant in discerning God's will (7:6–10), certainly prayed real (not pretended) prayers. He appreciated human love in mother and friends, 'loved' the Bethany trio, spoke with deep foreboding of the pain and persecution still to come.

John seems especially interested in Jesus' acuteness of mind and depth of insight, a facility of perfect humanity unclouded by prejudice, envy or contempt, a total intellectual sympathy that is a gift of love.

Such insight is emphasized at Jesus' first interviews with Peter, Nathanael, Nicodemus, the woman in Samaria. Jesus perceives the crowd's intention (6:15), the disciples' murmuring (6:61, 64; 16:17–19); and throughout proves a very keen debater. In John's record Jesus asked only five or six factual questions, though rhetorical, argumentative questions are his main weapon of debate. This admiration of Jesus' mind reveals forcibly how realistically John thought of Jesus as fully human.

It is a serious distortion, therefore, to suggest that Jesus walks through John's Gospel a foot above the ground. Yet it is not difficult to see what gave rise to such a comment.

Astonishing claims

For the claims made by and for Jesus in John's Gospel are truly breathtaking. At least one hundred times John draws attention to Jesus' unique relation to God as 'Son' (sometimes 'only-begotten Son') to the living Father. His existence before coming into the world is likewise insisted upon: he was 'before Abraham', 'in the beginning with God', 'came from God', 'proceeded and came forth from God', 'came from the Father'. The world was made by his agency; he is 'from above' and belongs 'in the bosom of the Father', having glory with God before the world was made. He is God's gift to the world—his only Son.

Over twenty times Jesus is entitled 'Lord'. He is the king of Israel, will die for the nation as the lamb of God who removes sin, drawing all men unto him, including 'the children of God scattered abroad'. This gives to Jesus universal significance; he is 'Saviour of the world' (4:42). He baptizes with the Spirit, raises the dead, bestows immortality. In his hand are the gifts of the bread of life, living water, light to walk by, freedom, entrance to God's fold. What greater claims could ever be made for any individual?

These claims are sustained by Jesus' sublime consciousness of being entirely one with God in mind and purpose. This is explicit in words like 'My Father is working still and I am working', which even his critics understood as 'making himself equal with God'. It is clear also in 'I and the Father are one'; 'He who has seen me has seen the Father'; 'I am in the Father and the Father in me'; 'as thou, Father, art in me and I in thee'.

The same consciousness prompts the declarations that to welcome and honour him is to welcome and honour the Father, as to reject and hate him is to hate the Father also; and that no one can come to the Father except through him, nor come to Jesus unless the Father draws him. Again, only those who know and love God will recognize who Jesus is.

Three times John insists that no one has ever seen God, in order to add that Jesus 'has made him known'. Jesus has seen the Father, and knows him, and will not deny it (6:46; 8:55). In Christ has been uttered the divine Word that reveals the mind and will of the unseen God to those who can hear it, and perceive who Christ is. At the opening verses of the Gospel Jesus himself is that uttered Word, with God from the beginning, and divine; at its close, its crowning testimony is spoken by Thomas—'My Lord, and my God'.

These are enormous assertions. In Jesus we see reflected God's mirror-image in human frame; God's glory is refracted through the prism of Jesus' mind and character in rays adjusted so as not to blind human eyes but to illumine them. This is the heart and height of John's own testimony: though no one has ever seen God, we have seen Jesus, whom to see is to see the Father. 'He who is nearest to the Father's heart, he has made him known' (1:18 NEB). 'We have beheld his glory, glory as of the only Son from the Father.'

Remarkable disclaimers

If the claims which John records, or makes, for Jesus are breathtaking, so is his emphasis upon Jesus' total subordination to his Father's will. The mirror that reflects God, the prism breaking the divine glory into bearable colours, is wholly without flaw. No ripple of self-will or shadow of disobedience distorts the divine image. Jesus reveals God by responding completely to every impulse of the Father's mind and purpose. He is, at every moment, and to every fibre of his being, the servant of God.

Though a Son, Jesus is someone 'sent', and the Father is 'he who sent me'; this is repeated at least forty times. The word used implies a courier, a spokesman, a representative, a messenger; 'apostle' derives from a different root-word, but bears the same sense of commission to a specific task (so Hebrews 3:1), and the same implication of being under orders.

This fundamental feature of Jesus' portrait, status, and vocation in John's Gospel is elaborated in a series of disclaimers so surprising that they are best listed in scriptural language:

▷ *Jesus is at all times under command:*

'This charge ['command' NIV] I have received from my Father' (10:18); 'I do as the Father has commanded me' (14:31); 'I have kept my Father's commandments' (15:10); 'I keep ['obey' NEB] his word' (8:55).

▷ *Jesus has no will of his own:*

'I seek not my own will' (5:30); 'I have come not to do my own will' (6:38); 'My food is to do the will of him who sent me' (4:34); 'I always do what is pleasing to him' (8:29).

▷ *Jesus has no initiative of his own:*

'The Son can do nothing of his own accord' (5:19); 'I have not come of my own accord' (7:28); 'I came not of my own accord' (8:42).

▷ *Jesus has no authority of his own:*

'I do nothing on my own authority' (8:28); 'I can do nothing on my own authority' (5:30); '[He who obeys] shall know whether the teaching is from God or whether I am speaking on my own authority. He who speaks on his own authority seeks his own glory' (7:17–18); 'I have not spoken on my own authority' (12:49); I do not speak on my own authority' (14:10); 'he whom God has sent utters the words of God' (3:34).

▷ *Jesus has no message of his own:*

'My teaching is not mine, but his who sent me' (7:16); 'I declare to the world what I have heard from him' (8:26); 'I ... speak thus as the Father taught me' (8:28); 'of what I have seen with my Father' (8:38); 'the truth which I heard from God' (8:40); 'the word which you hear is not mine but the Father's who sent me' (14:24); 'I have given them the words which thou gavest me' (17:8); 'I have given them thy word' (17:14); 'The Father who sent me has himself given me commandment what to say and what [or 'how'] to speak... What I say, therefore, I say as the Father has bidden me' (12:49–50).

▷ *Jesus has no judgment of his own:*

'The Father... has given all judgment to the Son' (5:22); 'has given him authority to execute judgment' (5:27); 'As I hear, I judge' (5:30); 'I judge no one. Yet even if I do judge, my judgment is true, for it is not I alone that judge, but I and he who sent me' (8:15–16).

▷ *Jesus has no work of his own:*

'My food is... to accomplish his work' (4:34); 'The Son can do only what he sees the Father doing; for whatever he does, that the Son does likewise' (5:19); 'The works which the Father has granted me to accomplish' (5:36); 'the works of him who sent me' (9:4); 'having accomplished the work which thou gavest me to do' (17:4).

▷ *Jesus has no power of his own:*

'Thou hast given him power over all flesh' (17:2); 'The Father who dwells in me does his works' (14:10); 'Believe the works, that you may know and understand that the Father is in me and I am in the Father' (10:38).

▷ *Jesus seeks no glory of his own:*

'I do not seek my own glory' (8:50); 'I do not receive glory from men' (5:41); 'He who seeks the glory of him who sent him is true' (7:18); 'the Father is greater than I' (14:28); 'greater than all' (10:29); 'Father, glorify thy name' (12:28); 'I am glorified in them' (17:10).

▷ *Jesus has no independent life of his own:*

'I live because of the Father' (6:57); 'As the Father has life in himself, so has he granted the Son also to have life in himself' (5:26).

▷ **All is God's free gift to Jesus:**

'The Father loves the Son, and has given all things into his hand'
(3:35); 'Jesus, knowing that the Father had given all things into
his hands' (13:3); 'They know that everything that thou hast
given me is from thee' (17:7).

A remarkable list, indeed! In such phrases, scattered throughout the Gospel, so constantly and so variously emphasized, we cannot fail to hear the accent of one utterly devoted, perfectly subservient, whose nature, mind and will do not in any slightest degree obscure the image or hinder the purposes of the Father he so completely obeys.

Irresistibly we are reminded of the moving words of Paul: 'Though he was in the form of God [he] did not count equality with God a thing to be grasped, but emptied himself, taking the form of a servant... humbled himself and became obedient...' The idea, and even the words, clearly echo Isaiah's memorable description of the coming servant of the Lord. In Isaiah's great chapter 53 the whole Church, following Jesus himself, saw prefigured the true Messiah, 'pouring out his soul unto death'—'emptying himself'—to redeem the world.

Even so does John describe Jesus, filling in the portrait by piling phrase upon phrase, quoting (at 12:37–41) the same prophetic chapter, and following it with the story of the servant washing the disciples' feet. In showing Jesus, 'the lamb of God which takes away the sin of the world', dying as the Passover lambs were being slain, John probably echoes Isaiah again: 'like a lamb ... led to the slaughter ... he makes himself an offering for sin ...'

This conception of the perfect Servant of the Lord dominates John's thought of Jesus. Real humanity, breathtaking claims, total subservience to the Father, combine in the portrait of One whose transparent life and devotion made him the ideal vehicle of divine revelation. Through him deity shone undimmed and undistorted into a world of darkness, suffering, and death.

Assured expectations

John's description of the incarnate Son as servant-Messiah does not exhaust his thought of Jesus. He has preserved numerous hints about the expected outcome of Christ's service, and the strong hope that sustained Jesus' own heart. The Baptist's word, 'He must increase ...' is not forgotten, nor Jesus' own clear understanding of his death as, like the planting of corn, about to 'bear much fruit' and reap eternal life. That his work on earth would continue is simply assumed; others would believe through the disciples' word, and lambs and sheep be pastored when he had 'gone' to God and to the Father's house, where the disciples could not yet follow. His 'going' is mentioned nine times, and where he is going to be, there eventually his servants will be.

This implies 'ascension' to the Father, foreseen in 6:62 and perhaps 1:51, and announced to Mary on Easter morning. Such a conception, linking Jesus' pre-existence in eternity past with his return to God's 'presence' in the eternal future (17:5), lends to the figure of Jesus a dimension of timelessness that sets him apart from all others.

Timelessness brings also universality. Despite Jesus' close involvement in Jewish affairs and conflicts, he is seen already as 'the light of men', not only of Israel, 'the light that lightens every man'. He is hailed as 'Saviour of the world'; he has sheep not of the Jewish fold whom he must gather; the approach of Greeks to see him signals that his hour has come to be lifted up and so to draw 'all men' to himself. From that moment, Jesus counsels the Eleven concerning the world's hatred, the world's need of witness, the world's coming judgment. Such foregleams of far-reaching future influence assume Jesus to be the man for all others.

A third expectation of the days beyond the cross concerns the presence in the world of the Holy Spirit, Christ's other self, the Spirit of truth. He will be 'another' comforter (counsellor) when Jesus leaves; the Eleven already know him, for he dwells 'with' them and will be 'in' them. He will not come unless Jesus goes to the Father, but at Jesus' prayer, and by Jesus' sending, he will take Christ's place on earth. This is the central theme of the Upper Room discourse—the indwelling of the Church by the contemporary Christ in all generations (see also 7:39; 2 Corinthians 3:17; Matthew 28:20).

This promise of the Spirit's coming sets the whole prospect of the future in a light somewhat different from that presented in Matthew-Mark-Luke. There older apocalyptic language about Christ's appearance on the clouds with angels, darkness, signs in the heavens, is still current. John appears to transmute the whole picture into a continuing experience of the presence of Jesus. But not entirely so: John, too, looks for a 'last day' of consummation, a further coming of Jesus (6:39, 40, 44, 54; 14:3; 21:22). Apocalyptic overtones linger too in the thought of 'the Bridegroom' (3:29; Matthew 25:6; Luke 12:35–36; Revelation 19:9), and the metaphor of the woman in travail (16:21–22; 1 Thessalonians 5:3).

The climax to the work of Jesus is further described in 5:25, 28–29: 'The dead will hear the voice of the Son of God, and those who hear will live ... when all who are in the tombs will hear his voice and come forth, those who have done good to the resurrection of life, and those who have done evil to the resurrection of judgment.'

For 'the Father ... has given all judgment to the Son' (5:22–27), and though he does not yet judge men, when he shall do so it will be justly, and shared with the Father (8:15–16). On one side, this 'hour' of judgment will be according to the word which men have rejected, the light they have refused, the obedience to the Son they have wilfully withheld, so incurring the wrath of God (12:48; 3:19, 36).

From another side, this 'day' or 'hour' will be—for those who accept Jesus—a resurrection to final security, when none will be lost, none perish (6:39–40; 10:28–29). In either case, Jesus will be finally vindicated, as the truth of his message is brought home to unbelievers, and the firmness of his promises is demonstrated to believers.

It is in such vindication, rather than in spectacle, violence, or punishment, that (for John) Jesus' ultimate victory lies. From the beginning of time, the light that is in Jesus has struggled with the darkness of the world, and has never been overcome (1:4). Now, in the final conflict with evil, which will cost Jesus his life, it is the prince and source of all evil who will be exposed and judged (12:31). Although the initial temptation story is omitted from John's record, when 'the ruler of this world' makes his final assault upon Jesus, he finds no handhold in him. Jesus dies, not as the victim of evil but in obedience to the Father (14:30). The ultimate victory is thus won already, in the soul of Jesus. He has overcome Satan, and the world, and will die in peace (16:33). It remains for the Victor only to inherit divine 'glory' (13:32; 17:1, 24).

Such was the assured outcome which John expected when the mission of Jesus was fully completed. A servant he might be, meanwhile, subordinate, obedient, humble, but in God's good time he would be recognized as the timeless, universal, contemporary, and coming, Christ of God, upon whom depends the destiny of all. This is Jesus, 'the Christ, the Son of God', in whom John would have us believe, that we might have life in his name.

6

Who Was John?

Johns abounded in Christian circles of the first century. Beside the Baptist and John the son of Zebedee, the apostle, we meet John Mark, the Elder of 2 John, 3 John, John the father of Peter (1:43), 'brother John', the seer of Patmos, and the 'presbyter John' ('elder') whom Bishop Papias, writing about AD140, could recall. Doubtless there were others, for the name was common. Which of them all wrote the fourth Gospel has never been decided. The book remains anonymous, as the author intended.

The traditional view

The name which printers place over the book in our Bibles enshrines the guess which became the accepted Christian tradition, that the writer was John the son of Zebedee, disciple, apostle, and styled 'the beloved disciple'. The theory is said to be supported by a certain 'Aramaic accent' about the book, by detailed descriptions of localities and customs, especially of Jerusalem, and by its close acquaintance with Judaism and rabbinic ways of thinking. The writer claims intimate knowledge of the circle around Jesus, their conversations, questions, motives, disagreements, misunderstandings, as himself one of the privileged inner few.

The author notes days and times, six waterpots, five barley loaves, one hundred and fifty-three fish, the perfume filling the Bethany house, the soldiers' reaction at Jesus' arrest, the cutting off of the servant's right ear, the servant's name, Malchus, and Jesus' robe 'without seam'. Such details suggest an eyewitness standing behind the book. Though much of the detail would be known to any Christian Jew of Palestine—and the son of Zebedee was a fisherman of Galilee, not a city man of Jerusalem.

The author speaks on large themes—the divinity of Christ, the coming of the Spirit, the relation of Christianity to Judaism—and does so with great authority. He exercises considerable freedom in handling the common tradition about Jesus, although existing Gospels express some things otherwise. But he does not assert apostolic authority, as Paul, where necessary, asserted his. The author of this Gospel simply assumes he will be listened to. Are we to explain this change, in a provincial fisherman, by his three years with Jesus and the experience of the Spirit, and seek no further?

It may be significant that the only 'John' mentioned by name throughout the book is the Baptist. It has been said that no one could have written the story of Jesus without mentioning John Zebedee, except John Zebedee. Some have found these arguments persuasive; others feel they are somewhat insubstantial to attribute such a book to such a man.

Why doubt the tradition?

It used to be argued that, since John made use of the Gospels of Matthew and Luke, and was acquainted with second-century Gnosticism, his Gospel was too late to be by one of the Twelve. Both reasons are questioned today. As for 'a Galilean fisherman's intellectual capacity', his being a business partner (Luke 5:10; Mark 1:20), and possibly a friend of the High Priest (18:15, assuming John was the 'other disciple'), should count for something, beside his years with Jesus.

John Zebedee was on the mount of transfiguration, and present at the raising of Jairus' daughter: could he have omitted such moments from his own story of Jesus? At 19:35, someone adds his own confirmation to what the author says: the words would be a most clumsy way of saying 'I saw it'. But could any one in that early Church presume to lend his own support to the apostle's testimony? The same must be asked about 21:24, whoever the 'we' may be; he who had leaned on Jesus' breast needed no man's confirmation when he told the story! (These closing verses are too obscure to provide argument: 21:22–23 implies that 'the beloved disciple' of 20 has died, yet 24 says he is bearing witness; 'who has written these things' may mean 'who caused these things to be written', note 19:22.)

These defensive interjections, confirming what the author says, do not suggest high apostolic authority behind the book, in the eyes of those who offer support. As we have seen, this defensive attitude to John's Gospel persisted in the Church to almost AD200. If the book was written by an apostle, the Church did not know that it was, or did not fully believe it, for over a century. Nor did the Church understand 'We beheld his glory...' (1:14) to mean only the original Twelve; as in 1 John 1:1–4, the whole Church in each generation is included in the 'we' of testimony, embracing also those who saw not, yet believed (20:29; compare 3:11).

Behind these nagging doubts lies a larger and vexing question: Who was this 'beloved disciple'? If we could read this Gospel for the first time, free of all preconceptions, we would answer confidently, 'Why, Lazarus of course!' Does not John say so three times—'He whom you love is ill... Jesus loved... Lazarus... See how he loved him...' (11:3, 5, 36)? And to confirm it, though the name of this well-loved Lazarus is mentioned at 12:1, 17, somewhat incidentally, it thereafter disappears, and 'the disciple whom Jesus loved' appears—and only then.

After this, 'the disciple whom Jesus loved' is seen in close intimacy with Jesus, reclining beside him at table in the Upper Room, and accepting the care of Jesus' mother as Jesus died (13:23; 19:26; 20:1–10; 21:7, 20—24; the home at Bethany with the two loved sisters would be a more convenient refuge for Mary at that moment, than would distant Galilee).

Nevertheless, from early times 'the beloved disciple' has been identified with John Zebedee, and assumed to be the Gospel's author, referring to himself under this title. To support this identification, it is urged that, if it be not so, then a disciple prominent in the other Gospels is totally absent from John's story. (But so are Matthew, James, Bartholomew absent from this Gospel, as Lazarus, Nathanael, are absent from Matthew-Mark-Luke; what can this prove?) It is argued too that 'the beloved disciple' is in this Gospel closely associated with Peter, as John is in the other Gospels. (Must we then assume that Peter kept only with John, and no other?) And it is urged that the presence of 'the beloved disciple' at the Lord's Supper proves that he was one of the Twelve. If we could be certain that only the Twelve were there, this might settle the question.

Some have thought that the temperament attributed to 'the beloved disciple' does not accord with 'a son of thunder' willing to call down fire upon offenders, and seek precedence over others (Mark 3:17; 10:35–37; Luke 9:54). Others note the tradition, late but persistent and fairly widespread, that John Zebedee and James died 'at Jewish hands' about AD44 (Acts 12:2). To the suggestion that this tradition grew out of Jesus' warning to the brothers (Mark 10:39), it has been replied that the warning would not have been preserved had the Church believed that John lived to write this Gospel late in the first century.

The testimony of the early Fathers is very confused, and much has to be assumed before it can be used as evidence—some who knew Ephesus never say John ministered there; a Bishop of Ephesus speaks of John as the beloved disciple who reclined upon the bosom of the Lord, and who was a priest and wore the sacerdotal breastplate. Here is no word of fisherman, apostle, or writer—can this be John Zebedee?

Irenaeus, a bishop in Gaul (130–200) formulated what ultimately became the Christian tradition, in the words: 'John, the disciple of the Lord, gave out the gospel in Asia until the time of Trajan' (Emperor, 98–

177). 'Disciple' was assumed to mean 'apostle'; 'gave out the gospel' was assumed to mean 'published a written Gospel'; and an apostle's immense age by that date was assumed to present no difficulty.

Concerning 'the beloved disciple' we are left with faint and fairly balanced possibilities (if we reject Lazarus), and no guidance on who wrote the fourth Gospel. Most students of the Gospel probably fall back upon their own feeling about the title. Some think it incredible that John Zebedee should ever refer to himself as 'the beloved disciple'—an audacious claim, presumptuous and arrogant; Paul could speak of 'the Son of God who loved me', but never of himself as the one Jesus loved; it is an affectation. Others can find in the title a grateful acknowledgement of Jesus' favour, intending no comparison with others. But is the comparison implied, nevertheless? (Still others have suggested a deliberately unkind contrast with Peter—the disciple who claimed to love Jesus!)

Other early writers deal with the authorship of John's Gospel very differently. Andrew, certain bishops, fellow disciples, are mentioned as collaborating in its writing; John was 'urged by friends and inspired by the Spirit'. Papias, Bishop of Hierapolis (near Ephesus) speaks (about AD140) of 'elders' reporting what apostles had said, naming 'the Elder, John' as a living and abiding voice. Later writers mention two tombs of 'John' at Ephesus, and even speak of the ordination of John by John.

Is this the clue to the Gospel's authorship? Some collaboration is hinted at in 21:24. The dual tone, Greek and Judaist, might well arise from double authorship. The 'arrogant', 'self-righteous' sound of the title 'the beloved disciple', when used by the author about himself, would of course disappear if applied to John Zebedee by an admirer and disciple, writing his teacher's memoirs.

Mark is believed to have written his Gospel to preserve Peter's preaching. The same relationship between 'the Elder, John' (of 2 John, 3 John?) and the apostle John—the essential teaching of the aged son of Zebedee being preserved by a younger pupil who delighted to call his revered mentor 'the disciple whom Jesus loved'—would be an attractive solution, and resolve many questions.

But that does not make it true!

Does it matter?

The strangest feature of this whole discussion is that the authorship of the fourth Gospel does not matter. There may be a certain pleasure in thinking we are reading the actual words of the aged son of Zebedee who lived with Jesus, if we can close our minds to the scantiness of the evidence. But no more than that is at stake. Whoever penned it, the

Gospel of John stands on its own feet, conveys its own clear message, and demonstrates its own authority.

The spiritual truth the book contains shines by its own light, not by its author's reputation. The inspiration of the Holy Spirit, self-evident to receptive hearts, may have come through apostle, elder, deacon or nameless believer, male or female. The book's historical veracity is equally unaffected by any question of authorship. The ultimate source of what John tells lies in the common tradition of the Church about Jesus, mainly shared by the other Gospels, and carrying the assent of hundreds who had met Jesus (compare 1 John 1:1–4—'we'; Luke 1:1–4). The author was not personally present at every point in the story, whoever he was (4:7–26; 7:3–9). If the common tradition did reach the author through John Zebedee, its veracity is trebly guaranteed.

By whatever title we prefer to honour him, there can be no doubt that John was one of the greatest thinkers, one of the outstanding leaders of Christianity in all ages. The achievement we described—his transplanting the gospel into new soil before its Judaist roots had entirely withered, and re-minting Jewish-Christian thought into the intellectual coinage of the wider world and the future—speaks for itself. We do well therefore to remain alert as we read. We miss much of his meaning if we assume everything to be obvious and familiar, approach the book in the half-awake 'mystical' mood we sometimes bring to devotional reading.

For John is a subtle and skilled writer. His double meanings tease the mind: 'Judas went out, and it was night' (in every sense); 'The Son of Man must be lifted up' (crucified? glorified? both?); 'Come and see' (where he dwelt? Who he was? What John has to show?). Dramatic moments startle attention: Pilate said 'Behold the man!', and a little later, 'Behold your king!'; Greeks from the outer world plead, 'Sirs, we would see Jesus'; a blind man thrusts his way through Jerusalem, his face plastered with clay, gathering behind him a tail of arguing sightseers, to wash in public!

Jesus, girded with a towel, kneels before his disciples and washes their feet. Again, he stands before an echoing cave-tomb, an over-awed crowd watching, silent and still, and he calls 'Lazarus, come out!' And Lazarus came, hands and feet bound, and face covered with a grave-cloth.

And John's depth of thought challenges reflection. He never dissolves historical events into mere symbols of deep truth, but it is the meaning of each miracle that interests him most. He allots seven verses to the healing of a blind man, and fifty-one to the discussion that followed it. He gives eleven verses to the feeding of the five thousand, and forty-two to drawing out its significance, on seven levels of interpretation.

So we must be vigilant. John will himself indicate the deep, saving truths he finds in the story; there is no need, no value, and some real danger, in inventing meanings of our own, 'spiritualizing' every detail. John's thought is rich enough, in all conscience, for most of us to digest. And sweet enough to enjoy!

In the end, of course, the value of John's Gospel to ourselves will depend, not upon who wrote it, but upon the sincerity of our hunger for eternal life, and our willingness to believe that Jesus is the Christ, the Son of God, in order to obtain it. Those who earnestly seek will find the book to be the very word of God to them. Those who have already found it so, need not be told how illuminating, refreshing, and strengthening, John's Gospel is.

Exploring
the Book

1

John's Introduction—Jesus As Seen By Others

John 1:1–51

John announces his great subject, Jesus, as he was seen by himself and by others, summarizing their impressions in nineteen or twenty titles which men have accorded him.

The evangelist's testimony   John 1:1–5, 9–14, 16–18

A magnificent beginning, spoken for the whole Church ('we' 14). Deliberately echoing Genesis 1:1, John identifies Jesus as the eternal 'Word' who formerly shared the united life of the Godhead. 'With God', here, means literally looking, or moving, 'towards' God.

He was, in the beginning of time, active in creation, when God spoke and what he said happened. Every living thing owes its being to the divine Word. Things 'came to be', but he was there, already, the source of all life and light; so Colossians 1:1–17; Hebrews 1:1–3. Thus already in creation, the Word strove through the centuries against the darkness, never yielding, never overtaken. It is a stupendous claim: Jesus was from eternity the rational and moral light of humankind, 'the light that lightens every man' (4, 9).

John is saying that all true light in human experience derives from the eternal Word. However dimmed or distorted by mistake, misunderstanding or malice, all that is good, all that is true, is prompted by the eternal Christ, and guarded by him so that it is never totally extinguished (5). This mind-stretching idea reflects some Greek thinking about the reason and morality that leaven human life.

But John steps beyond all human philosophy in testifying that in due time, the inherent 'reason' behind all things, the very Word of God, came among us. He came to his own realm, but was rejected by his own people. Nevertheless, upon all who recognized him, and believed that he is what his name declares, he conferred the right and 'authority' to become children of God. That opportunity is no natural right (John says), nor the privilege of any one nation, but is bestowed in response to faith.

What is more, the divine Word 'appeared on the scene' (literally) as flesh. John frequently emphasizes Jesus' real humanity. In flesh the Word 'set up his tent' among us, as a passing traveller, though the phrase recalls too the tabernacle in the wilderness, where also Israel saw the divine glory (*shekinah*, recalling Exodus 33:9; 1 Kings 8:10–11; Psalm 85:9). That glory, shining in Jesus, was such as only the unique Son of God could inherit (14).

Verse 14 neatly corresponds to verse 1. The Word was divine, he appeared in flesh; he existed in the beginning, he came to be in time; he was within the fellowship of the Godhead, he lodged for a while among us; he was the expression of divine thought ('the Word'), he uttered that thought in a human life.

Out of the fullness of his divine and human nature we have all received a succession of favours, one grace piled upon another, grace renewed, adapted, multiplied, as our needs change. God fulfils himself in many ways, lest one grace repeated should surfeit the soul.

'Grace' occurs in John's Gospel only here; 'truth' occurs twenty-five times, so answering Pilate's famous question, 'What is truth?' Grace without truth may be misled, descending to sentiment, condoning evil. Truth without grace can be censorious, insensitive, ruthless, unforgiving. In Jesus, grace and truth are balanced perfectly, and complete.

In verse 17, John begins the contrast of the Christian message with Judaism, of Jesus with Moses, which will occupy him for some time. Law, a necessary discipline and condemnation of evil-doing, was given through Moses; it is excelled, and superseded, by the inexhaustible grace and unassailable truth so freely available through Christ to transform evil into good.

John's personal testimony to what he has found in Christ (12–17) reaches its climax in the resounding claim of 18. That, unlike pagan idols, the true God is invisible, was a cardinal truth of Judaism. Isaiah's question, 'To whom then will you liken God?' had been echoed more recently by a famous teacher, Ben Sirach, 'Who has seen him and can describe him?' It had been asked again in that first century by Philo, and many cultured 'God-fearing' Gentiles crowding the synagogues, weary of polytheism, were asking it urgently. There was scarcely a more timely or more pertinent question.

In reply, John declares that Jesus has the authority ('the only Son'), and the intimate knowledge ('reclining on the Father's breast'), to unfold God's purpose, express God's mind, explain God's character—in John's word, to 'expound' God. Paul, travelling a world of idols and temples, had likewise felt the force of the question, 'What is God like?', and had made the same answer: Christ is the 'image' of the invisible God (Colossians 1:15; 2 Corinthians 4:4).

It is a staggering claim; only familiarity robs it of its wonder and excitement. But then John's entire testimony to Jesus is enough to make each new reader pause on the very threshold of his book. Even the language is unfamiliar. We rarely call Jesus 'the Word', even today, except in a few older hymns, nor does John use the title again in the Gospel. Why did he use it here?

Partly, no doubt, because the idea of a divine word, expressing eternal wisdom, was familiar to the Jews. Such a divine word came to the prophets, revealing God's mind about the nation's life. By his word God had created the world, the spoken word conveying his power (so Isaiah 55:11; Psalm 29). And all things happened 'according to God's word'—as he said it should. To Jewish minds, therefore 'the divine word' was the utterance of God's thought, the vehicle of his power, and the assertion of his sovereign purpose. John means that Jesus was all that!

But some Greeks, too, spoke of the 'word' (using John's term) meaning the expression of rational thought (not a meaningless noise). Such rational thought ruled the universe; there was reason behind all things, which it was the business of philosophy and science to explore and express. Reason had created the orderly cosmos out of the original chaos of matter, and still held all things together and in order. Such reason, moreover, was the light within the human mind, the gleam of moral insight within the human conscience. To Greeks who thought like this, John's opening paragraph would be at least interesting.

John is using current language, to contend that what such Jews and Greeks were struggling to *describe*, Jesus *was*: the self-communication of God in thought, power, and will; and the inward light of men made in God's image. What startled Greeks, and made the Jews stumble, was John's further pronouncement: 'The Word became flesh . . .'

By so introducing Jesus, John has also announced the leading ideas of his Gospel: the background of eternity, the unveiling of God, Jesus' divine sonship, the reality of revelation, God's gift of grace and truth, and the crucial importance of believing.

(We return, now to verses 6–8, 15, which plainly interrupt 1–18, and may have been added on later revision. Without them, 1–18 in the original partially resembles a Greek hymn, in poetic couplets, addressed to Christ the Word. A fascinating possibility—but no more.)

Suggestions for group discussion:

1   Modern descriptions of Jesus emphasize 'the man for others', 'the Christ in our fellow man', 'our brother and our friend'. In the light of John's testimony, does this humanizing of Jesus reduce Christianity to sentimental friendliness?

2   Many so-called agnostics are simply unable to accept the biblical images of God as fearsome, angry, almighty, an implacable lawgiver and judge. In reply, some suggest a greater emphasis upon Jesus as the only adequate 'living image' of God. Others argue that that is precisely the claim that alienates people of other faiths, and provokes inter-religious strife. What does the group think?

The Baptist's testimony   *John 1:6–8, 15, 19–34*

What the Baptist thought of Jesus would have great weight for Jewish readers, since as we shall see (3:22—4:3), his influence in Jewry deepened and widened through several generations. He represented the emergence again in Judea, after long silence, of the revered voice of prophecy, and his martyrdom at Herod's hands only added to his spiritual status in the eyes of pious and patriotic Jews. That is why Mark's Gospel, and the usual pattern of apostolic preaching (Acts 10:37; 13:24; see 1:22), begin the story of Jesus with a reference to the Baptist's ministry as forerunner of the Christ.

John now follows their example, but omits all else about the Baptist's message to concentrate upon his testimony to Jesus. He was not 'the light', but was sent from God to bear witness to the light of Christ; he insists continually upon the superiority in rank and priority in time of the one who is coming (15, 30).

Public religious teaching in Judaism was the prerogative of priests and rabbis; baptism of proselytes was reserved to lawyers, who issued certificates to converts. Levites (19) served as temple police, musicians, guards and the like. The Baptist possessed no official credentials. Hence the challenge of 22, 25.

Verse 19 begins a momentous week (note 29, 35, 39, 43; 2:1).

Controversy concerning the Baptist's significance and authority still rage in John's day, lending special importance to his denials (20). Elijah (21) was widely expected to return (Mark 9:11; Malachi 4:5), according to the Mishnah in order to restore order. He was thought to be waiting in heaven to anoint the hidden Messiah. The Baptist's manner, clothes, appearance in the wilderness, and message of judgment all deliberately imitated 'the spirit and power of Elijah' (Matthew 11:10, 14; Mark 9:12–13; 8:27–28).

'The prophet' (21; 7:40) refers to 'one like unto Moses', another expected forerunner of Messiah (Deuteronomy 18:15; Acts 3:22; 7:37). All the Gospels identify the Baptist as 'the voice of the herald' (of Isaiah 40:3), but only John shows the Baptist himself citing the words. The Baptist was 'a voice'; Jesus was 'the Word'.

The Baptist's answer to the challenge in 25 diverts the argument to the unrecognized Messiah already present in that generation (and in that audience? note 29). The Baptist's subordination to the Messiah is mentioned again. Rabbis were permitted to require of a pupil every service demanded of a slave, except the removal of a master's sandals.

The next day's testimony is very significant (29, compare 36). 'Lamb' was commonly used of sacrificial victims (see 1 Peter 1:19; Acts 8:32). 'Takes away' means literally 'continually lifts and carries', 'bears away'. 'Sin', here, is sinfulness itself, not just any accumulated sins. 'Of the world' looks far beyond Jewry. More words of Isaiah seem to be in the Baptist's mind: the servant of the Lord was 'led as a lamb to slaughter'; on him the Lord laid the iniquity of us all; he made himself an offering for sin, and bears the sin of many (Isaiah 53).

Jesus' priority is mentioned yet again (30, 15). Then the Baptist confesses he was ignorant of his kinsman's messiahship until the promised sign of the descending dove revealed it (31–33; compare Isaiah 11:2). By the Spirit's remaining on him, Jesus was enabled to baptize with the Spirit. John assumes that we know that the Baptist was gathering a community prepared for the Messiah by repentance and baptismal purification. The dove was sacred throughout Palestine, and a symbol of the Spirit in rabbinic writings, following Genesis 1:1–2. (The idea of gentleness, in contrast with the Roman eagle, and of innocence as in Matthew 10:16, has to be imported into the Baptist's words, not extracted from them.)

This promise of a baptism with the Spirit is ascribed by Matthew, as well as John to the Baptist, and by Luke to the risen Lord (Acts 1:5). Water, also, was a symbol of the Spirit following Isaiah (44:3), Ezekiel (36:25–26), and Joel (2:28; compare John 3:5; 7:38). The notion of a 'baptism' with the Spirit is not therefore unnatural.

It is of course quite possible that the Baptist should make this promise, echoing these prophets. But Matthew and Luke regard his 'promise' as really a forecast of judgment by Spirit (upon the souls of men) and fire (purging the nation and the land; Matthew 3:11–12; Luke 3:16–17). It would not be surprising if, after Pentecost, the Church understood the promise differently; especially if Acts 1:5, 8, is meant to show Jesus himself re-interpreting it.

The climax of the Baptist's testimony is in verse 34. The title 'Son of God' implies both messianic status and divine sonship (as at 1:49; 11:27; 20:31, and frequently in the other Gospels). Though John does not say so, it echoes the Father's words to Jesus at his baptism, 'You are my beloved Son'. John evidently expects us to know this. By John's time, the Church was familiar with the thought that a close 'filial' relationship underlay Jesus' awareness of being Messiah. The Baptist's own thought was probably nearer to that of Psalm 2:7; 89:26–27.

The Baptist's testimony, as John gives it, seems far too 'Christian' for a desert prophet before Christ's ministry had even begun. That Jesus is Lord, the coming one long-promised, altogether worthy to be served, wholly prior and pre-eminent, the lamb of God, possessor and bestower of the Spirit, and Son of God, makes quite an advanced Christian confession to be heard between the Testaments. Nevertheless, the Baptist's father was a priest, and normally priests' sons trained for priesthood—a teaching office—with the Old Testament for a their textbook. Certainly behind the Baptist's words lie Old Testament suggestions and language. Moreover the nature and status of the Messiah was being widely discussed in Jewry.

That our author, John, and we ourselves, find in the Baptist's affirmations depths of thought which only subsequent experience would unfold, need not be denied. We need only to be careful not to read back into the Baptist's Old Testament echoes all that these same prophecies came to mean in due time, as Jesus expounded them and later experience confirmed them.

Suggestions for group discussion:

1   In the light of the Baptist's promise, renewed by the risen Lord, and the baptismal experience of Jesus, do modern Christians give sufficient attention to the connection of baptism with the experience of the Spirit?
2   Words like 'witness', 'confessing (Christ)', 'testimony', are used of the Baptist nine times, and in John's Gospel twenty-two times. Does the group agree that the widespread unbelief of our time is the result of the moral and intellectual climate, or is it due to the lack, the confusion, the incompetence, of Christians 'witnessing' to their faith?

The disciples' testimony   *John 1:35–51*

Further tributes to Jesus, using additional titles, complete John's introduction. At the same time Jesus is gathering followers.

The first two (35–40) hear the Baptist repeat, apparently in private, the testimony of 29. They immediately follow Jesus, who opens conversation with them. The disciples' enquiry is said to imply a polite request for an interview; 'Rabbi' was the usual respectful address to any religious teacher, and is used to the Baptist himself at 3:26.

Jesus' reply (39) neatly summarizes the invitation of the whole book; it is repeated by Philip at 46. Mention of the precise time (four p.m. Roman style) suggests personal reminiscence. The only named participant, Andrew, begins at once to be prominent in John's account, as the first named Christian disciple.

The transfer of followers from the Baptist to Jesus, with the Baptist's knowledge and apparently upon his initiative, is very significant for the relative status of the two teachers.

The testimony of this first pair lies in their immediate attachment to Jesus, as plainly worthy of allegiance. Andrew's testimony goes further, naming Jesus as Messiah, and bringing his brother to Jesus, as later he would bring others (6:9; 12:22). 'First' in 41 may mean 'before doing anything else', or that he was first to bring anyone to Jesus. Some early copyists understood John to mean 'early in the morning', 'first thing', after a night with Jesus.

'Son of John' (42) at once individualizes and personalizes Peter, as does the immediate conferment of a new name. This is characteristic of Jesus, who never lost sight of the individual in the crowd, or of the person in abstractions like 'all men' or 'humankind'. 'Looked' (42) implies close scrutiny, piercing insight (2:25; Mark 10:21; Luke 22:61). Together with the new name, it suggests that Jesus read Peter's character as impulsive, emotional, and therefore vacillating. 'Cephas' (Aramaic) and 'Peter' (from Greek) both suggest rock-like strength, signifying what Simon will become in Jesus' hands. A new name marking a spiritual crisis in one's life was familiar to Jews, as Abraham, Jacob, Gideon, Barnabas and Paul illustrate.

This story of Peter's call is very different from Luke's, with the miraculous catch of fish and the promise about becoming a fisher of men (Luke 5:1–10). It is probably best to regard John's story as describing Peter's first interview with Jesus, and Luke's as a second, when after trying and failing to be rock-like, Peter learns to let Jesus take charge, even of his fishing! This would explain the (otherwise inexplicable) passionate cry, 'Depart from me, for I am a sinful man, O Lord.'

Peter's later denial of Jesus, under sudden stress and his 'insincerity' towards Gentile Christians (Galatians 2:11–14) show that the rock-like character did not happen overnight. The fact that the Church found it possible to believe the tradition of his flight from persecution at Rome until he met Jesus making for Rome 'to die again' confirms this view.

In truth, Peter's kind of strength lay, not in unshaken consistency but in the devoted tenacity which struggled with weakness, failure and fear all through his discipleship, but would not let Christ go. He made no other profession but to love Jesus, right to the end, and his testimony lies in the immediate capitulation implied in 42. Through storm or fair weather, through success or failure, Peter is Jesus' man from that first interview onward (see also commentary on 21:4–19).

The fourth disciple to respond and testify is Philip, and again the initiative is taken by Jesus. This Philip (he is not to be confused with Philip the deacon and evangelist, Acts 6:5; 8:5) is mentioned in the other Gospels and Acts as a mere name in the list of apostles; in John's record he is mentioned again in 6:5, 7; 12:21; 14:8. This difference of emphasis is hard to explain, unless some personal affinity lies behind it; the mention of Philip's birthplace again suggests personal reminiscence.

Philip's response is simply assumed; he testifies that Jesus was foretold by Moses in the Law, and by the prophets. Nazareth is mentioned, and Joseph named as Jesus' father (without qualifications). At the time, and still when John was writing, Philip's testimony constituted an immense claim: Jesus is the climax of Israel's long history, the fulfilment of agelong expectations.

Nathanael, like Peter, is mentioned as sufficiently known to the readers, though he is referred to again only in 21:2, and nowhere else in the New Testament. Any identification with someone else, as Bartholomew, is mere guessing. Yet he seems to have continued with Jesus 'from the beginning' (if Acts 1:21–23 may be applied to him). But in complete silence, so far as the records show! Nevertheless, he received one of the greatest tributes Jesus paid to any man (47).

Nathanael voices the persistent Jewish prejudice against Jesus, as coming from Nazareth, a town almost unknown (not mentioned in early Jewish literature), insignificant, provincial, and of mixed population (in 'Galilee of the Gentiles'), and so despised (compare 7:41). But Philip's perfect reply, 'Come and see', that is, 'for yourself!'—the best remedy for preconceived opinions—brings him face-to-face with Jesus. Jesus' warm praise, and swift character assessment, instantly gains his attention.

Jacob (the first 'Israelite') was by reputation crafty. His own father complained of his guile; his brother and his father-in-law could have done so too, and even Hosea recalls it centuries later. Jesus contrasts Nathanael, a true Israelite, without craftiness, with the old untruthful Jacob.

Nathanael's astonishment (48) was due, not simply to Jesus' knowing that he valued integrity, but to something even more striking. The fig tree, with its drooping, tent-like branches, was a favourite place for privacy, especially for prayer (Micah 4:4). Christ's compliment, and the reference to opened heavens and angels ascending and descending, revealed that he knew the very subject of Nathanael's meditation—the story of Jacob at Bethel (Genesis 28:10–22).

Once again Jesus has revealed his insight into another's mind and heart. Nathanael responds with a heartfelt 'Rabbi, you are the Son of God! You are the king of Israel!', and in reply Jesus promises a Bethel experience for all his followers ('you', 51, is plural).

When this promise is to be fulfilled is not explained. That Jesus is himself a link, a sort of Jacob's ladder, between heaven and earth is true, but hardly relevant. The title 'Son of Man' (recalling Daniel 7:13; see Matthew 25:31; 26:64), and the mention of angels, may hint at Jesus' return in glory, though at this point such a reference seems very remote. A promise that they shall see opened heavens and angels ascending and descending to welcome the Son of Man when he returns whence he came, seems as probable an explanation as any that has been offered (compare 6:62; Acts 1:9–11).

Thus John has introduced his subject, Jesus of Nazareth, the divine Word, 'God', the light of men, agent in creation, made flesh, the only Son from the Father/Son of God, the prior one, the altogether worthy, Christ/Messiah, the revealer of God, the Lord, the coming one, the lamb of God, the bearer of sin, the baptizer with the Spirit, Rabbi, the fulfilment of prophecy, son of Joseph, king of Israel, and Son of man. All are titles or descriptions of far-reaching religious importance, together defining an altogether unique religious status. It is a large enough subject for any author, a well of spiritual enrichment for all who read with care, and faith.

Suggestions for group discussion:

1   The varied means by which these five disciples were introduced to Jesus illustrate well different methods of personal evangelism—a teacher, a family, a friend, Bible study… The group might study each instance, think of parallels, some from their own experience, evaluate each method, and gather any lessons indicated.

2   The titles and phrases applied to Jesus by John or recorded by him, were all current in Jewish religious thought. Today they need careful explanation, and make little impact. Can the group think of more familiar titles or phrases by which to introduce Jesus to their contemporaries—Führer, Guru, Captain, 'our President' (in republican areas), Liberator, Ayatollah, 'Lord of the dance'…? (Titles used in modern hymns may help.)

2

Christ's Self-manifestation in Deed and Word

John 2:1—4:54

John's first main section recounts six apparently miscellaneous incidents. Jesus had been in Judea with the Baptist, but intended to go to Galilee (1:29, 43); in 2:1 he was in Cana, near Nazareth, and then moved to Capernaum 'for a few days'. With Passover approaching, Jesus went to Jerusalem, where (John says) he 'cleansed' the temple, did his signs, and talked with Nicodemus. 'After this' Jesus returned to the Jordan in Judea, near where the Baptist was ministering, but when comparisons were provoked he set out again for Galilee, lingering however for two or possibly three days in Samaria (4:43). Then again he visited Cana.

At first sight a seemingly casual, purposeless itinerary. Besides, Matthew-Mark-Luke and the accusations made at Jesus' trial show that the cleansing of the temple occurred at the close of the ministry. (No Gospel suggests it took place twice.) That Nicodemus came by night to see Jesus seems to imply that official hostility made the visit dangerous—so early in John's story?

It is fair to conclude that John has assembled incidents from varied occasions to illustrate a theme, not to detail Christ's movements. In four of them, the contrast between Jesus and Judaism, already foreshadowed in 1:11, 17–18, 30–33, 47, 51, surfaces in regard to the temple worship, the Law, prophecy, and racial exclusiveness. In the two Cana miracles, contrast with Judaism is admittedly less obvious, but it is suggested. Tentatively, therefore, we accept that Christ's manifesting himself and his mission, by words and deeds, in contrast with Judaism, governed John's selection of incidents in this section of his book.

Jesus and Judaism—wine and water   John 2:1–12

The deed at Cana was essentially a nature-miracle, a normal grape-harvest hastened. It cannot reasonably be dismissed as an invention of

John to illustrate the superiority of Christian experience over insipid Judaism; details like six waterpots, Mary's intervention, the place and precise timing, the secrecy, and the comment that the miracle marked a stage in the disciples' faith, would all be pointless in such an invented tale.

The secrecy must reveal the motive for the miracle, which was simple kindness. The arrival of Jesus with five disciples strained the resources of a village home to the point of public shame—marrying, when they couldn't afford to feed their guests! The servers had to know, the disciples knew, probably later; the master of ceremonies did not know what had happened, and was left in his bewilderment; the village gossips never knew.

John explains, for Gentile readers, how water came to be abundant in a Middle Eastern village home: it had been saved up for well-mannered (or ritual) purification on the great occasion. The idea that Jesus created one hundred and twenty gallons of wine, to keep the whole village drunk for a week, is ludicrous; the servants drew water (9), and the miracle occurred between the drawing and the drinking.

Mary learned of the need—was she assisting in the catering?—and her reaction was naturally to turn to Jesus, upon whose resourceful-ness she had long relied (note 5). Jesus' response was certainly not disrespectful; 'O woman' recurs at 8:10 and again at 19:26, both moments of great care and tenderness. But the words (as literally translated) 'What [is] to me and to you?' are significant. They might be rendered, 'What has that to do with you or me?', expressing reluctance to interfere in a private domestic crisis, but his action does not bear that out. A similar Hebrew expression served to discourage a request—'What do you and I have in common?' (2 Samuel 16:10 NIV), compare 2 Kings 3:13; Mark 1:24; 5:7). Mary did not take the words to mean refusal, and in view of the outcome Jesus' words amounted to 'You had better leave that to me.'

Their significance lies in the change of relationship, from that of a dutiful son subject to his mother's will to that of a man with a high vocation. Henceforth Jesus must watch for his 'hour' and its duties (4), an idea that recurs nine times (see commentary on 12:23). A similar sense of detachment underlies 7:5. Mary reappears only at the crucifixion, after the few days at Capernaum. According to Mark 2:1; Matthew 4:13, this important trading centre, some twenty miles from Cana, became Jesus' 'headquarters', 'his own city' (Matthew 9:1; compare 11:23–24).

So far, the story is a charming rural idyll illustrating the human sympathies of Jesus, and so it has been read at countless Christian weddings. Whether any theological meaning should be read out of or into it, is less clear. The water of Judaism being replaced by the rich wine of the gospel is one possible 'interpretation', with Mark 2:22 to justify the metaphor. John sees the incident as a 'sign' of the power and 'glory' of Christ, confirming the disciples' incipient faith, and he sets it first in a series of events which contrast Christianity with Judaism.

Jesus did, in fact, bring the 'best wine' of Hebrew faith 'last', after centuries of negative, and somewhat joyless Judaism. John's contemporary, Philo, had written that the wine which Melchizedek brought for Abraham (Genesis 14:17–18) had been miraculously produced from water, and had called Melchizedek 'the word, the winemaker'. Was John (like Philo) glancing at the Greek myth which made Dionysus discoverer of the vine, who regularly turned water into wine for his worshippers at Corinth (from the fifth century BC)?

We may wish that John had made his meaning clearer, but he may have been confident that the Cana story would attract, and echo in, both Jewish and Greek minds without further emphasis.

Suggestions for group discussion:

1 Everything about this story implies Christ's approval of life's good things—feasting, good fellowship, celebration, simple pleasure, not excluding sexual joy and happy marriage. Yet Christianity retains its reputation for austerity, repression, self-denial, 'puritanical' censoriousness. Can the group explain why, or how to correct it? Is Christianity essentially life-enhancing, or life-inhibiting?

2 Some detachment from parental direction and family expectations, in order to fulfil one's personal vocation in freedom, often faces young people in these days. Experience suggests that it causes pain and disruption in Christian families as often as elsewhere. Can the group suggest guidelines for parents, and for Christian young people, for handling this problem?

Jesus and the temple   *John 2:13–22*

For illustration of Jesus' attitude to the Judaist temple system and its worship, John turns to the dramatic challenge which Jesus enacted at the close of his ministry. Because of difficulties of travel with animals, and the possibility of their rejection by the priests when they arrived, worshippers bought sacrificial victims from official traders at the temple. Hebrew coins only were accepted for temple dues or donations, so money-changing at the temple was unavoidable, such coins being illegal elsewhere. Exchange rates were fixed by the temple authorities.

This double monopoly caused popular rioting both before and

after the time of Jesus. Such sacrilegious profiteering prompted Jesus' quotation of Jeremiah's protest, that priests had made the temple 'a den of robbers' (Mark 11:17). John, however, draws attention rather to the secularization of the precincts—'a house of trade', 'a shop' (Moffatt)—the effect of which was to exclude visitors and pilgrims from the court of the Gentiles.

These grievances, felt by many, explain how Jesus, acting alone, could take such vigorous action; the authorities, fearing another riot, leave him alone until later. The whip of cords (15) was literally a twist of rushes, but in Acts 27:32 it is strong enough to tow a boat. Doubtless Jesus used a rustic halter snatched from a tethered animal. The immediate reaction of the disciples was to recall, perhaps to each other, Psalm 69:9, possibly enjoying and certainly excusing Jesus' strong indignation as a fulfilment of prophecy.

The Jewish authorities, scandalized by Jesus' behaviour demanded some sign of his authority for so acting, but receive only a somewhat ironic promise that he will provide one in due course. When the Jews destroy their own temple by such desecrating misuse (or by bringing Rome's vengeance upon themselves?) he will replace it 'in three days'—'in a couple of days', 'in no time at all'. (The time mentioned is no more to be understood literally than the promise itself; Jesus did not rebuild the Jerusalem temple at any time.)

But, as so often in this Gospel, Christ's critics chose to misunderstand the Hebrew idiom (compare Hosea 6:2), and argue about the time it took to build Herod's temple. John's own comment (21–22) is clearly stated to be hindsight; it does not follow that he has misread Jesus' meaning, as some suppose. Orthodox Jews would not miss the double reference in the story to the Passover (13, 23), when every pious household diligently cleansed its own home as Jesus now did his Father's house. Dissident Jews would see in the story a direct attack upon the whole sacrificial system, which they themselves abhorred.

Other things Jesus said and did suggest that this latter view was not far wrong. It is true that Jesus attended the temple festivals, which involved sacrifices, as the first Christians, including Paul, also did (Acts 3:1; 5:25; 21:23–26). But Jesus prophesied the temple's destruction (Mark 13:1–2), repeatedly cited Hosea's words 'I desire mercy *and not sacrifice*', spoke to the woman of Samaria about true worship without fixed place or form, preferred to call the temple 'a house of *prayer*', and used its colonnades for *teaching*. In consequence, Christianity soon repudiated sacrificial worship altogether.

This had certainly happened by the time John's comment was written. Temple, priesthood, sacrifices, had been swept away—by the Romans: the sign promised had been given. The centre of Christian worship had moved out of the synagogues also, to become the two or three gathered in Christ's name, with the Lord's table, and the living Christ 'in the midst of them' (see Matthew 18:20). Thus, even for Jewish Christians, in place of the ancient shrine of Israel, selected by David, erected by Solomon, restored by Herod, there had arisen a 'holy temple in the Lord' into whom Christians were built 'for a dwelling place of God in the Spirit', 'a spiritual house ... a holy priesthood, to offer spiritual sacrifices' (Ephesians 2:21–22; 1 Peter 2:5).

This is the hindsight to which John refers. And since Paul's time, if not earlier, the title freely given to that 'living temple', the Church of Christian believers, indwelt by the Spirit, was 'the body of Christ'. The language itself is older: Athenians spoke of 'the body of citizens', Philo and the Stoics both spoke of the body as a temple; but for Christian hearts, the words kindled memories of Christ's broken body, and the eucharist, and the experience of the indwelling Christ, to give it altogether new meaning.

Though the explanation is involved, it probably does not misrepresent John's meaning, as it certainly does not misrepresent what actually happened in the apostolic Church. The cleansing of the temple, for good reasons, during Christ's ministry, had prefigured the removal of the temple, in due time, and its replacement, for Christians, by the living, worshipping 'body of Christ'. That 'living temple' had come into being at the resurrection of Jesus and the subsequent Pentecost. Christianity had (by John's time) left Judaism's reeking rituals far behind, substituting a form of devotion which presented the Christian's body as a living sacrifice, holy and acceptable unto God, in a spiritual—because reasonable—worship (Romans 12:1).

To this point the progress of John's thought is fairly clear, but as we shall see it is characteristic of John that his thinking can proceed on more than one level at once. To prosaic Western minds the relation between one level and the other is sometimes unclear—as here, 'the temple of Christ's body' and the body raised from the dead (21–22) seem to involve a confusing play upon words. More seems to be meant than that the body which is the Church and the body which was raised coincided (roughly) in time. Without the resurrection there would have been no Church, and it is the risen, living Lord who is the life of the Church. Is that what John means?

(Similarly, the Scripture in 22 may look back to 17, or possibly to Old Testament prophecies of Christ's resurrection: Psalm 16:8–11; Isaiah 53:10–12, for example.)

Suggestions for group discussion:

1   Does the group agree that the interpretation offered is 'the only

plausible meaning that can be attached to verse 21'? Or can the group offer a better one?

2 Early Christians rejoiced in an awareness of drawing near to God in Christian worship, whereas Judaism tended to keep worshippers 'outside the veil'. Look up Romans 5:2; Ephesians 2:18; 3:12; Hebrews 10:19–23; Matthew 27:51. Then let the group consider whether our modern worship conveys that deep sense of privileged 'access' to the presence of God.

Jesus and the Law   *John 2:23—3:21*

Words rather than deeds provide John's third topic on which to contrast Judaism and the gospel, a searching conversation followed by far-reaching comments.

Again Jesus' clear insight into human character is emphasized (25; compare chapter 1). He understands the shallowness of faith which depends upon 'signs' regarded as spectacles instead of as acts of compassion and power which convey a meaning. Hence, though 'many *put their trust* in his name', he did not *trust himself* to them. From Nicodemus' opening words (3:2) he appears to be an example of those described in 2:23.

Jesus brushes aside the flattering introduction to address the central issue between himself and the Pharisees. They sought moral reform and acceptance with God through ever stricter application of Jewish Law in innumerable regulations; he offered new life, direct from God— 'from above'.

The confrontation was dramatic. Nicodemus was old, devoted to traditional Judaism, a member of the Sanhedrin (3:4, 10; 7:50–51). Jesus was younger, untrained, officially unrecognized, and with a radically new message. Judaism at its most earnest faced Christianity at its source, Jesus, each offering in God's name a way of salvation. Why Nicodemus came by night is not explained; convenience, or leisure, would hardly deserve notice; secrecy, in view of some danger in associating with Jesus, is the likelier reason.

The 'kingdom of God' is introduced without explanation, as already familiar not only to the speakers but to John's readers. One must be reborn even to 'see' it, whether born 'a second time' (4) or 'from above' (6, 12) or both, is not clear (compare Matthew 18:1–4). As so often, the saying is misunderstood in literalist fashion, and Jesus explains that by rebirth he means 'of water and the Spirit', and by truly 'seeing' the kingdom he means 'entering' (or experiencing) it.

In this context, to be 'born of water' can refer only to the Baptist's 'baptism of repentance', a rite marking a new beginning, reformed and purified, with ideas like Psalm 51:2, 7; Zechariah 13:1; Ezekiel 36:25–26, and the precedent of Jewish proselyte baptism, behind it. Jesus was sending Nicodemus back where he himself had begun, to an act which, when applied to Jews, deeply offended the Pharisees (Matthew 3:7–9).

Such a new beginning, penitent and self-purifying, opened one's whole experience to the life-renewing Spirit, which the Baptist had promised Messiah would confer. So to be 'born of water' would imply also being 'born of the Spirit'. It is the addition of 'and the Spirit', exemplified in Christ's own baptism, which transforms the Baptist's rite into Christian baptism, the sacrament of new beginning.

John has already noted the difference between being born 'of the will of the flesh', with a nature merely human and adapted to this world, and being born 'of God' with a nature adapted to life in God's will (1:13; compare 6:63). There John was speaking of Jesus, here he speaks of anyone seeking the kingdom, in whom the Spirit creates a new nature adapted to new life (see Ezekiel 36:26–27).

Here lay the fundamental difference between Judaism and the new gospel. Judaism offered rules, by which the old human nature could be disciplined to good living, given the will and the moral strength. Jesus offered renewal, a new nature in which goodness would be inherent, a life inspired with the adventurous, unpredictable freedom of the wind (verse 8—the same word, in Greek, as 'Spirit').

For inspired people are the very antithesis of well-regulated, law-bound people. 'Where the Spirit of the Lord is, there is freedom' as Paul insisted, and 'For the law of the Spirit of life in Christ Jesus has set me free from the law of sin and death. For God has done what the law . . . could not do' (see 2 Corinthians 3:17; Romans 8:2–3). Christians are all leaves before God's wind (8); 'you hear the sound of it' (was it a rough night in Jerusalem?) but you know not whence or whither. So the inner working of the Spirit is unseen, though the effects are clear to all (see 1 John 2:29; 4:7; 5:4–5).

Centuries of Judaism had not brought Jewry to experience the divine inward rule—'the kingdom of God'. Improvement in teaching, fresh applications of the Law, more intense discipline and austerity, all are insufficient while human nature remains unchanged. A new nature, a new life-source and motivation, are necessary for a radically new lifestyle. Nothing less will save Jewry ('you' in 7 is plural)—or humanity.

Nicodemus asked 'But how?', the wistful question of the old in every generation. Jesus replied 'You must' (5), 'and you can' (7–8) for the Spirit so moves. When the question is repeated, Jesus rebukes 'a teacher of Israel' who does not understand this elementary distinction between the fleshly and the spiritual life. The rebuke neatly echoes Nicodemus' opening flattery!

It is impossible now to be certain where the conversation ends, and John does not tell us its result, though later we learn that Nicodemus demands a fair hearing for Jesus (7:50–51), and at the end shows allegiance to Christ, late but just when it was most dangerous to do so (19:39).

Meanwhile, somewhere between 11 and 16 John pauses to comment. He wishes others to share the life that begins in rebirth, and so seeks to make clear at this point how the gift is given, and the divine love that makes it possible. And the consequences of refusing it. In addition, this confrontation of Judaism with Christianity continued into John's own day, the Jews still failing to understand or to accept. John would explain why.

These two purposes govern the comments of 11–21. But while the 'I' of 11, 12 is plainly Jesus, the 'we' who speak, know, have seen, are rejected, must be the apostolic Church (as in 1:14; 1 John 1:1–4). And the 'you' in 11, 12 (plural here as in 7) must mean the Jews generally.

Jesus appears to speak to Nicodemus on behalf of all those who would eventually be born again, and to anticipate the rejection of their testimony by Jews who would continue to voice Nicodemus' objections. Past record mingles with John's later experience. By 14–16 John is speaking of Jesus in the third person ('believe in him' not 'in me'), and using past tenses ('has ascended' . . . 'has not believed' . . . 'loved darkness'). A few ancient copies show that this double timing (recording what happened in Jesus' time from the viewpoint of a later time) was noticed very early. The phrase 'which is in heaven' (AV) added to 13 could not have been used that night in Jerusalem.

John's explanation of Jewish unbelief lies in 12–15. The earthly things which Jesus and his followers know and have seen, but which Nicodemus and his fellow Jews in John's time still refuse to believe, are the 'earthly' stories of Jesus' coming, life, and death. Rejecting these, the Jews cannot begin to grasp the 'heavenly' meanings behind them, the offer of new life through new birth, the gift of the Spirit, for example.

But then, no one could explain these heavenly things but one who has access to heaven; and no one has such access, except the Son who descended from there and 'has ascended' (at the time John wrote). The firm denial that any one has hitherto been admitted to these heavenly secrets was probably directed against mystics and apocalyptic writers such as the author of 'The Secrets of Enoch', a prophetic manual very popular from the first century BC.

This insistence upon Christ' ascension involves a curious pun; John uses 'lifted up' to mean crucifixion (like Moses' lifting of the serpent on a pole) as the first stage in the ascension to heaven (so 12:32–33; 8:28;

note Isaiah 52:13, of the suffering servant of the Lord). When Israel in the wilderness was plagued by venomous snakes (Numbers 21:9), as a Jewish commentator said, 'they received a token of deliverance . . . [the serpent of bronze] . . . For he who turned toward it was saved, not by what he saw, but by . . . the Saviour of all' (Wisdom of Solomon 16:5–7).

The momentous result of the offer of new birth, a share in heavenly secrets, and the death and exaltation of God's son, is 'that whoever believes in him may have eternal life'. John never speaks of eternal sin, fire, punishment, but he does speak seventeen times of eternal life, always as a present possession. To fail to understand, like Nicodemus at this time, was to miss the opportunity of real life now and immortality hereafter, neither of which could Judaism offer.

Turning, finally, to how the gift of eternal life is given, received, or lost, John offers some of the maturest fruits of his long reflection on the gospel. He traces all back to the Father's love. Any idea that Jesus died in order to make God love us, or to enable him to do so, is ruled out completely. And so is any idea that his love was for 'the elect', whether Israel, or Gentile believers; it was love for all humankind, for 'the world'. That was the motive which prompted God to 'give up' (literally) his only Son.

The Son is here God's 'gift', and the divine intention behind the gift is wholly to save. The scope of that loving initiative is universal ('whoever'), though as always love becomes effective and successful only in those who believe and accept it. He, she, who so believes escapes all condemnation; he, she, is 'saved'.

Nevertheless, refusal to believe constitutes self-condemnation 'already', not in some distant future, because unbelief forfeits now all that God's love offers. This is self-judgment. It reveals a preference for what is dark and evil. The light of the offered gospel exposes an already existing predisposition, whether towards good or towards evil (19–20).

This moral predisposition, a kind of self-predestination, is mentioned frequently by John. The guileless, such as Nathanael, welcome the light as it comes; those who are 'of the truth' hear Christ; those who are willing to obey readily understand the teaching; 'he who is of God hears the words of God: the reason why you do not hear them is that you are not of God' (18:37; 7:17; 8:47).

It is not by prior divine ordaining that any one is judged, according to John; it is self-judgment by being the kind of person you are. Christ as little comes to pass judgment on the world as the sun rises to cast shadows, though the judgment (like the shadows) is the inevitable consequence of the light he brings. Salvation is no question of merit or deserving. God loves all, offers salvation to all, but those who 'love darkness ... who do evil ... who hate the light' refuse God's invitation. No one can ever deserve Christ: but we show what we are by the way we respond to him.

Altogether a marvellous paragraph, too familiar to be appreciated properly. The New Testament has few (if any) more important passages. It contains the very heart and promise of the Christian gospel: the divine initiative of the eternal love of God towards all humankind; the focusing of God's overmastering purpose to save in the free gift of his Son as Saviour; the resulting offer of new birth, the endowment of the Spirit and immortality for all who choose to believe in Jesus; the eternal issues of life or 'perishing' that depend upon that choice; and in consequence, the brilliant light that is thrown upon all human goodness and evil by the presence of Jesus within human history.

John's pause for reflection was well worth the time and space that it consumed!

Suggestions for group discussion:

1 While appreciating fully the depth and richness of 3:16–21, would the group want to add any particular truths, ideas, challenges or duties to it, before agreeing that 'it contains the very heart and promise of the Christian gospel'?

2 Modern Christians have heard much about the promise of the Holy Spirit, and some have experienced more of his power in their lives. Sometimes emphasis has fallen upon strange, even bizarre 'signs'; sometimes upon strong emotion. Does the group think that, with all this, the average Christian life attains to all that Jesus meant by being born of the Spirit? What else would the group look for, in a 'Spirit-filled' life?

Jesus and prophecy   *John 3:22– 4:3*

In recording the Baptist's testimony to Jesus (1:6–8, 15, 19–34), John drew attention to how often the Baptist emphasized the priority of Jesus, in time and status, to himself. The point was important, because of the place the Baptist came to occupy in Jewish thought, up to and long after John's time. To his own generation, Jesus was first and foremost a prophet (4:19; 6:14; 7:40; 9:17; Mark 8:27–28). John shows that both the last of the Jewish prophets, the Baptist, and the first of the 'Christian prophets' were ministering at the same time, in roughly the same area along the southern Jordan, practising the same rite of purification. Inevitably, they appeared as rivals.

Jesus was drawing the greater crowds, making more converts (3:26;

4:1). An unnamed Jew questioned the value of this baptismal purifying, evidently disturbing some of the Baptist's disciples. Somewhat jealously they drew their master's attention to Jesus' success, reminding him that earlier he had spoken well of Jesus. They appear to imply that people are becoming confused as to which prophet, and which baptism, has the greater authority.

The Baptist replied that success and status are God-given (27). He had always disclaimed being the Christ—he is only 'groomsman' at Messiah's wedding, glad to be present, but without envy of the bridegroom. He is but the morning star, inevitably fading as the sun rises (the terms of 30 are said to be astronomical).

Again, John pauses to comment; 31–36 closely resembles and develops the thought of 16–21; its language could not be expected from the Baptist. The theme is still the relation of Jesus to the Baptist, and to the long line of human spokesmen for God, the prophets. They, including the Baptist, belong to the earthly, historical development of Judaism; Jesus, coming from heaven, is superior to all. He has seen, and heard, what he testifies to, although none receive his testimony (again later experience colours the language). Not all reject, however; those who do believe add their own witness to God's truthfulness, since Jesus utters God's words (note the converse, 1 John 1:10).

Other prophets, including the Baptist, were Spirit-inspired to the degree needed for their tasks. One Rabbi judges the 'measure' of the Spirit given to each by the length of his writings! To Jesus the Spirit is given without limit, so that everything he says is God's word. What is more, the Father loves the Son (35; 5:20), and out of that loving relationship has given all things into the Son's hand, including the gift of eternal life for all who believe. And with it, God has given the authority to confirm the divine judgment that follows automatically when men or women refuse the Son all obedience. There remains no doubt that, great as the Baptist was upon his own level, Jesus is infinitely greater. Nevertheless, to avoid any semblance of rivalry, Jesus leaves the Jordan for Galilee (4:1–3).

Strangely, 3:22 and 4:1 are the only statements in the New Testament that Jesus ever baptized. The supposed 'correction' in 4:2 is very clumsy: peculiarities in the Greek may point to a copyist's comment. The 'correction' is also quite pointless, since if the disciples baptized in the presence of Jesus, his approval and authority must be implied. The words spoken to Nicodemus, his own baptism, and the immediate adoption of the rite by the Church, all confirm Jesus' approval of baptism (4:1 resembles Matthew 28:19 'make disciples, baptizing them . . .')

John obviously valued the Baptist's testimony to Jesus, and his humble, self-effacing attitude. Yet time after time John compares his importance unfavourably with that of Jesus:

▷ *he is not Messiah, not Elijah, not 'the prophet', not the light, not the bridegroom*

▷ *he is only a voice, a witness, a lamp shining 'for a season' (5:35), a friend of the bridegroom*

▷ *he must decrease as Jesus increases*

▷ *he did no miracle (10:41), did not recognize that Jesus was Messiah until the sign was given, made fewer disciples than Jesus, and directed at least some of them towards Jesus*

▷ *he is not worthy to become shoe-slave to Jesus, and his testimony about Jesus is less important than that of God, and could be dispensed with (5:34, 36)*

▷ *his baptism of Jesus is not described, only the descent of the dove, which was for the Baptist's benefit*

▷ *he is later than, inferior to, and altogether less important than Jesus.*

Taken alone, this insistence suggests almost an animus against the Baptist. It is in fact a deliberate reply to exaggerated claims for him. The earliest Christian preaching had linked the Christian movement to the baptizing prophet—'beginning from the baptism of John' (Acts 1:22; 10:37). Jesus had submitted to baptism at his hands. Luke records the existence of disciples of the Baptist in far away Ephesus a generation later, with Apollos, who had learned of the Baptist at Alexandria in Egypt (Acts 18:24–25). By the beginning of the third century, some were claiming that the Baptist was the true Messiah, founder of Christianity, originator of baptism, and teacher of Jesus. In reply, some Christians began to rank the Baptist among false prophets.

John is resisting earlier forms of this unfortunate exaggeration of the Baptist's place in the Christian story. The prophet is not disparaged, or repudiated; he is shown as a faithful, self-denying witness to his great master and Lord. But John insists that his ministry was preparatory, provisional, and of necessity transient. He was a waning star, a burning and a shining lamp 'for a season'. Jesus, not the Baptist, was manifested as crown and fulfilment of Jewish prophecy.

Suggestions for group discussion:

1   Does the group think that John has served the Baptist well, or ill? Why?

2   From the beginning, rivalry has divided and hindered Christian

workers and churches; sometimes from excessive loyalty to individual leaders; sometimes from claims to more effectual sacraments; sometimes from varying conceptions of 'success'. Can the group think of examples of these, or of other causes? What does this passage teach us about such rivalry?

Jesus and the Samaritans   *John 4:4–42*

In this charming vignette, Christ's self-manifestation by deed and by word are closely interwoven. The tactful approach of Jesus to this lonely stranger, making himself a suppliant to initiate conversation; the historic setting of Jacob's well and nearby Shechem; the heart-searching discussion with its profound undertones; the surprise of the disciples and the response of the Samaritans, are all features which lend high drama to a simple tale of personal contact with Jesus which renewed a soul. The key to its significance lies in a comment, almost an aside, by John: 'Jews have no dealings with Samaritans' (9). But Jesus does!

A woman whose sins have left her life drained of loyalties, affection, friends and love (15) comes far and alone through a parched landscape (35), to meet another weary and thirsty soul (6, 7), who offers her perpetual refreshment (14). The words 'If you knew . . . you would have asked . . . and he would have given . . .' (10) carry us to the heart of spiritual experience, by three basic steps. The utterances about God as Spirit, and worship in spirit and truth, carry us to the ultimate meaning of all devotion.

Yet it is not in details that the significance of the story lies for John. The space he allots to it, and its position among these contrasts with Judaism, show its continuing importance. Whether 4 implies divine necessity or (as elsewhere) simple convenience, the visit and its outcome reveal once more the far-reaching superiority of the gospel over Judaism.

For 9 exposes the total failure of Judaism to come to terms with these unorthodox 'half-Jews', their nearest neighbours. The estrangement arose from the age-old rivalry between the ancient tribe of Ephraim and upstart Judah. It was given religious 'justification' by the story of incoming pagan peoples after the fall of northern Israel (2 Kings 17:24–41). Under Greek and Roman occupation, Samaria had been more susceptible than Judah to foreign influence, though she clung jealously to the ancient Israelite tradition etched into her very landscape in sacred sites and memorials. She formed, in the first century, an unorthodox, rival fringe of Judaism, alienated, suspected, and despised.

By the time John wrote, Christianity had largely succeeded where Judaism had not even tried. Jesus had commanded (35) and initiated the great mission to Samaria which Luke describes (Acts 8:4–25). In consequence, contrasted with the narrow, self-righteous, nationalist attitude of Judaism, Jesus was manifested as 'the Saviour of the world' (42). To those to whom Judaism had nothing to say, Jesus reveals himself as Jew, prophet, Messiah, universal Saviour (9, 19, 25–26, 42). It is noteworthy, too, that 'woman' occurs thirteen times in the story. Several of these occurrences are inevitable, but the word is underlined firmly in 9, 39, and especially 27. For here also Jesus is crossing frontiers. Rabbis condemned much talk with women, even to avoiding their own family in public places.

'The sixth hour' (probably noon), her coming alone, and her story, suggest the woman is shunned. As a French scholar, Godet, remarked 'Jesus knows well that one way to gain a soul is to ask a service.' In reply, the woman raises the central issue (9). About AD65 it was decided that Samaritan women were best treated as 'always unclean', which would exclude any sharing of food vessels with them. That formal rule merely enforced existing attitudes and practice.

'Living' (spring, not well) water was a familiar metaphor for life, wisdom, salvation, the Spirit. Another saying (10–11) is misunderstood literally, then explained. Travellers often carried leather 'buckets' (11); verse 12 is full of Samaritan pride. Jesus promises inexhaustible inward resources, perpetually refreshed, perhaps echoing Isaiah 58:11. In 7:39 these resources are mentioned again, but as flowing out to others. With 13–14 compare 6:35, 50. The woman's reply is hardly 'flippant', nor merely unbelieving: 'if only it were true—how I wish it was!' probably strikes her wistful note.

If the conversation was to be prolonged, propriety would prompt 16. But it also opens the way to explaining how the woman may obtain her wish. For there are things to put right. At once she perceives that Jesus is a prophet, whom she cannot deceive (19, 29). The sudden introduction of the subject of worship is entirely appropriate, not an evasion. In the presence of a prophet, the main issue between Samaritans and Jews, the validity of the original temple site at Gerizim, or the later Zion (where Josiah of Judah had centralized worship) would immediately arise (2 Kings 23:8, 19–20). That implied also the further question as to which priesthood, which system of worship and festivals, had divine authority (note Luke 9:51–53).

Jesus' reply, pursuing 2:13–21, is radical and final. Rivalries about sites, shrines and systems all disappear when the spirituality of true worship is understood (21–24). When John wrote, 21 had been literally fulfilled. Hellenists, and other dissident Jews, would welcome

Jesus' declaration (compare Acts 7:48).

'Our father Jacob ... our fathers worshipped on this mountain ... worship the Father ...'—Jesus abrogates all traditional sectarianism; the 'validity' of worship rests not on its place, antiquity, or form, but on its object and its spirit. Salvation comes historically through (literally, 'out of') the Jews' experience of divine revelation, but in Christianity it becomes available to all who offer what the Father seeks, true worship. The mark of such worship is, that it matches the nature of God as Spirit, and not the prejudices, or the preferences, of the worshippers.

'God is spirit' (24) summarizes Judaism's unique theology in three words; 'the Father seeks' summarizes the Christian gospel with equal terseness. The woman suggests, probably again wistfully, that the coming Messiah will resolve all such questions; a vague messianic hope lingered in Samaritan thought. The answer of Jesus constitutes a moment of supreme self-manifestation, made to an individual, to a woman, to a Samaritan, and a sinner! 'I who speak to you am he.' (For similar revelations made to individual women, compare 11:25; 20:16.) *X*

In Greek, that reply has the form 'I am, I that speak to you', recalling 'I am the bread of life ... I am the resurrection and the life', and the name by which God was made know to Moses (Exodus 3:13–14). 'I am' occurs in John some eleven times, and is said to carry the accent of deity. This can be exaggerated, for sometimes the phrase bears quite ordinary meaning, as when we use it. In a few instances there is a solemnity about Jesus' utterance (as here), which would not be lost upon Jew, Samaritan, or even some pagans (Isis, and other gods, were thought to use this formula of divine speech).

The arrival of the disciples breaks the tension of verse 26 and releases the woman. She, heedless of her original intention, and for greater speed (or as pledge of her return?), leaves her water jar and hurries homeward with her news, her testimony, and her momentous question (29). Meanwhile, the disciples are unusually tactful! This time it is the disciples who understand Jesus too literally (27, 33). Doing God's will and work is for the true servant not merely duty but his daily food and nourishment (34).

Verse 35 quotes a rural proverb on patience, which Jesus contrasts with counsel to be ready for every opportunity—as he had been—even for one lonely, sad woman in unpromising circumstances. As each takes his opportunity, whether simply to sow, or just to reap, together (as another proverb says) they will surely be rewarded. The work of God is best done, not by brilliant bursts of isolated genius, but by the accumulated influence of faithful souls each seizing partial opportunities and leaving the final harvest to God.

Matthew (9:37–38) preserves a saying very like John's verses 35–38, but spoken apparently on a different occasion. This raises the question whether John has added here what Jesus said elsewhere, as a fitting comment on the Samaria incident, in the light of those who entered into what Jesus had begun, and reaped so rich a reward in Samaria some years later (Acts 8:5–25). It is just as possible that Jesus foresaw the future harvest of his present sowing, and John remembered his words.

The immediate harvest of only a couple of days' sowing in Samaria is movingly described: that field was indeed already white and ready for reaping (39–42). The faith which springs from others' testimony becomes firsthand upon personal acquaintance with Jesus (42), another fine statement in line with the book's declared purpose (20:31). The substance of the Samaritans' confession of faith, 'the Saviour of the world', goes further than the main point of the story. That is, plainly, Jesus' superiority to Judaism in bringing truth and salvation, convincingly, to those beyond the fringes of prejudice and rejection.

Suggestions for group discussion:

1 What does this story teach about personal evangelism? Who are our 'Samaritans', the near neighbours we profess to love but rarely reach out to?
2 How far dare we carry the principle laid down in 4:21, 23, that the place, the form, the system of worship, however hallowed by age or authority, do not matter if the worship be as God desires, 'in spirit and in truth'? Does this cancel all argument about liturgy, tradition, sacramental versus charismatic, Orthodox versus Quaker, Christian versus Muslim worship?

Jesus and the alien   *John 4:43–54*

John closes this section of his book by bringing Jesus back to Cana, where it began, for a second 'sign' (46, 54). The brief story is remarkable enough to demand to be told: a healing, practically a gift of life (47, 49, 50–51, 53 emphasize this), accomplished at a distance, without sight of the patient, by word only, and for a child (49). And performed with every sign of reluctance, overcome by earnest entreaty and sublime faith (49, 50).

Yet John omits so much in Jesus' story that is remarkable, and that he knew (20:30); we know that he is arguing a case. Why then did he find room for this particular incident? We can claim only probable answers, avoiding dogmatism.

The first probability concerns 'an official' (46), or 'a . . . royal official' (NIV), 'an officer in the royal service' (NEB), 'a royal' (literally, implying a person). The word is rare, the meaning vague: a relation of the king (Herod)? a courtier? (note Luke 8:3), a soldier in the king's bodyguard? Josephus, the Jewish historian, uses the word of Herod's troops in Galilee, and this is the likeliest meaning, Herod being the only 'royal' ruler in Palestine. No one close to Herod was likely to be a pious Jew.

Mark (3:6; 12:13) records opposition to Jesus from 'Herodians'; Herod murdered the Baptist, and (probably for this reason) Jesus refused to speak to him (Luke 23:8–9), though Herod had long wished to see Jesus and to witness some sign by him (Luke 9:9; 23:8). This background may well explain Jesus' rebuke when one from the Herod circle arrives in Cana from Capernaum asking for a miracle. For the rebuke is not addressed to the man individually, but as representing a group, a type: 'you' in 48 is plural—'Unless you [Herodians] see signs and wonders, you [all] refuse to believe.'

The second probability concerns the relation of this story to that in Matthew 8:5–13; Luke 7:1–10. There a soldier pleads for a servant or slave, paralysed or dying, by coming himself or sending Jewish elders, urging Jesus not to come but to speak and heal from a distance, which was done, and the time noted with special care. This was at Capernaum; John speaks of the miracle as at Capernaum, though performed from Cana. The difference between 'son' and 'servant' in Greek is slight and ambiguous. The likenesses in the two accounts outnumber the differences. If we judge all three Gospels to be telling the same story, then the 'royal person' was a centurion seconded to Herod's service, and therefore a Roman.

In that case, in this story, Jesus has again crossed a boundary, whether to the Gentile world of Rome, or just to the half-pagan world of Herod. Neither step would Judaism have cared to take. When orthodox Jews sought converts among Gentiles (Matthew 23:15), it was to make them Jews by religion and nationality, not to make them pious Gentiles. Here, in Jesus, the gospel steps beyond the Samaritan half-brother to the secularist, half-pagan Herodian, or more probably to the totally alien Roman, from a world quite outside Jewry. To that 'foreign' society also, Jesus offers life, as Judaism could not, and would not if it could.

Capernaum was some twenty miles from Cana, and 'the seventh hour', understood as one o'clock the following afternoon, involves inexplicable delay. Almost certainly the seventh hour of the fever, the crisis hour, is meant. The coincidence between that timing and Jesus' word of promise, is unaffected; and it deeply impressed the household.

A small puzzle remains unresolved. The saying in 44 is cited in Matthew 13:57 and Mark 6:4 to explain Jesus' rejection in Galilee; as John quotes it, it seems to imply that 'Jesus' own country' was Judea, and Galilee his refuge, despite 1:45; 7:41–42, 52; 18:5, 7; 19:19. Does John mean that Judea and Jerusalem, the centre of power, was the proper native place for the world's Messiah, and not provincial Galilee? That seems unlikely, but what then does he mean?

John's first main section has made its point fully and forcibly. In deed and word, the way of Jesus is seen to be in every respect superior to the way of Judaism. Jesus enriches life, erects a living temple of believing souls, offers a new nature for new beginnings, possesses great prophetic authority, inspires a higher quality of worship, oversteps every boundary of prejudice and racial discrimination. Judaism cannot rival Jesus—he is the Saviour of the world, the very Son of God.

Suggestions for group discussion:

1 John's argument is not that Judaism is wholly wrong, false, useless, evil, and only Christianity is true and good, but that Jesus fulfils, excels and supersedes all that Judaism can offer. Should this be our attitude, too, to Islam, Buddhism, Communism, and all other 'faiths' and philosophies?
2 Jewish exclusiveness towards Samaritans and foreigners was originally protective, striving to preserve traditional truths and standards, to guard the rising generation from the pressures of alien occupation, and so to ensure the nation's future. It became self-righteous, inward-looking, legalistic, intensely proud. What does this teach us about the duty of the Christian towards 'the world' and its pressures?

72

3

Christ's Self-manifestation in Conflict

John 5:1—12:50

In John's second main section, Judaism's fulfilment in Jesus is further illustrated, while the note of contention grows considerably sharper, and the conflict more public. The long, involved arguments to which each incident gives rise are wholly typical of this Gospel, and carry its main teaching and message.

God's dependent servant   John 5:1–47

In Jerusalem for an unnamed feast, Jesus finds a chronic paralytic lying beside a healing spring. The Dead Sea Scrolls have probably preserved the spring's true name, long confused, 'Beth Esdathaim'; 'is' in 2 implies that the story took form while Jerusalem still stood. Possibly because of the man's self-pitying manner, Jesus asks with wry humour if he wanted to get well. With the command to take up his mattress and walk, Jesus healed him and outraged the Jewish authorities; for it was the sabbath.

The Jewish Mishnah lists thirty-nine tasks forbidden on the sabbath, including carrying 'furniture'. Challenged, the man reported Jesus' words, and 'the Jews' replied, with a touch of contempt, 'Who is the fellow who said this?' Jesus had slipped away, and the man could not name him; his excuse was accepted, for it was Jesus they were after.

Later, finding the man in the temple, Jesus warned him to sin no more. Jesus did not hold the Jewish doctrine that every sufferer had sinned, but of course it was true of some (Mark 2:5; John 9:1–3). Learning Jesus' name, the man reported it to the authorities, probably out of fear (so 11:46; contrast 9:33–38). When Jesus was then challenged, he produced a new justification for his action, not Scripture precedents (Mark 2:25), or simple compassion, or an accusation of hypocrisy (because his critics dealt more kindly with their valuable beasts, Luke 13:10–17), but with the claim to do as God does, as his agent and representative. For 'God is working up to this (sabbath) moment' (17, literally).

Some Jews would have agreed that though God rested after creation, he remained always active; Philo, for example, said, 'as the property of fire is to burn and of snow is to chill, so the property of God is to create'. Others pointed to the sun's rising, rivers flowing, birth and growth all proceeding on the sabbath. Rabbis denied that such divine 'working' broke the sabbath, since 'the whole world is God's private residence'!

Nevertheless, Jesus' claim to act as God does, to share his freedom and privilege, seemed clear blasphemy (compare 8:58–59; 10:36). Together with his calling God 'his own Father' (literally), it implied (the Jews said) a claim to be 'equal with God' (recall 1:1–2; Philippians 2:6). That claim, and Jesus' answer—that the Son depends totally upon the Father, and the Father bears witness to the Son (19–30, 31–47)—is the key to the following discussion. For John, this is the point of the story, Jesus' sevenfold denial that he could, or would, ever act independently of the Father.

The far-reaching significance of this argument is fully explored in our introductory paragraphs, 'Remarkable disclaimers'.

John's immediate purpose was to reply to any current suggestion that Christians believed Jesus to be 'a second God', 'a demi-god', or 'a man exalting himself to be God'. Jesus does not claim equality with God: he is (here) the perfect, transparent, totally subservient servant of the Lord, whose life, words and conduct reflect without distortion the character of God, and convey without hindrance the power of God. Thus in him God is perfectly made known.

Jesus' denial of all personal initiative (19) again recalls Philo: 'the firstborn Son imitated the ways of the Father'. The 'greater works' (20) are those detailed, raising the dead, giving life, judging men. Raising the dead and giving life (21) are unexpected here, but the miracle under discussion was a restoration of life to paralysed, 'dead' limbs. Jewish daily prayers described God as 'quickening the dead', the divine prerogative (compare 2 Kings 5:7). The Mishnah declares that three keys are in God's hand, and are given into the hands of no representative: the keys of rain, of the womb, and of resurrection. With the last-named was joined, in orthodox Jewish teaching, the prerogative of final judgment.

Here (20–27) similar prerogatives are bestowed upon the servant-Son, not as inherent privileges but as gifts, with the honour that attaches to them. Even so, these are immense claims, vindicated (as John knew) in the experience of believers, who possessed the life that is eternal, and had escaped the judgment by passing forgiven from death to life.

Verses 25–29 are a little confusing until we notice that 'and now is' occurs in 25 but not in 28. Already, in Jesus' time and in John's, the spiritually dead (or paralysed) hear the voice of the Son and live, because the Son, like the Father, is a source of life (25–26). In future, even more wonderfully, those who have died will likewise hear the voice of the Son, and come forth to judgment, because like the Father the Son now has authority to judge. Judgment, and the throne of judgment, were popularly associated with the coming Messiah, 'the Son of man' (see Daniel 7, especially 13–14, 27).

That judgment will be on the basis of 'works', that is, character and behaviour (29; compare Matthew 25:31–46; Romans 2:6–11; 2 Corinthians 5:10). Verse 24 seems to contradict this: John apparently means that 29 applies to those who have not already passed from death to life. In 3:18, those who actively reject the gospel are condemned already thereby.

Jesus repeats that his imparting life and executing judgments in this way do not rest upon his own authority or his own will. He acts as the Father's voice directs (30, so 19; 8:16). His judgment is therefore never arbitrary, prejudiced, or self-assertive: its integrity and impartiality are assured by his own self-effacement.

Turning next to the testimonies by which such claims are supported, Jesus acknowledges that, under Jewish Law, self-testimony is always suspect (31). He has another witness to call, one whose truth is beyond question, namely God (32 with 36). But then, his hearers had themselves sent enquiries to the Baptist, and through prophetic lips they heard the truth about Jesus. He reminds them of this, that they might be convinced, perhaps, by their own enquiries! For the Baptist had been a burning, shining lamp, about whom they had been greatly excited—for a time!

Not that Jesus really needed such human testimony. God continues to bear witness (32, 36), and his testimony must be of far greater weight. This divine authentication is to be seen partly in the works which the Father has granted Jesus to accomplish, such as healing a paralysed man with a mere word. Though Jesus treated with caution a faith which rested upon signs and wonders (2:23–25; 4:48), yet the power demonstrated in his deeds, and their nature as acts of compassion, did provide evidence of the divine origin of his mission (so 36).

That testimony was confirmed further, by the inner voice of God in those who know him and love him (37–38, 42). His critics did not know God, nor have his word within their hearts, nor yet the faith to recognize one whom God has sent (see 7:17, 28). The Jews, it is true, possessed the Scriptures, and studied them diligently, believing that in the Law was the promise of life. But they studied Scripture as they listened to the Baptist, without learning anything. The written word was revered without the indwelling word to illumine it; the ancient voice of God they held sacred, the contemporary voice of God in Jesus, they would not listen to. So they did not find the truth they sought, nor the life. Both were to be found only in Jesus, as the Scriptures themselves testified; and him they rejected.

Probing further these inner attitudes, Jesus isolates the root cause of Jewish hostility in Jewish pride. The word 'Jew' (*Judahite*) means praise, glory; a pun underlies 41–44 (and 12:43, Romans 2:29; this pun appears to be a familiar point in Christian replies to Jewish criticism!) Those who seek continually for men's praise, and for self-glorification, understand and welcome others engaged in the same scramble for attention and adulation (43). They cannot understand, or value, self-effacement, the readiness to be accounted nothing if only God may be glorified (41, 43, 44). John implies that Jews of his own time are no different.

So they failed, and still fail as John writes, to understand that Jesus was not claiming equality with God, or seeking glory for himself, but only the Father's approval of his service (44). For him, God's praise completely outweighed the world's fickle approbation—and its opposition.

Was the crowd becoming uneasy under this heart-searching analysis of their motives? The argument closes with an assurance that Jesus had not come to accuse, any more than to condemn (45; 3:17). They have an accuser already, the same Moses upon whom they set their hopes. For the Law itself finds all at fault. If they had truly believed Moses, they would believe Jesus, since Moses wrote of him (46; 1:21—the prophet like unto Moses—1:45).

So the long debate returns to the testimony of the Scriptures. The present tenses in 39, 46–47 ('You search . . .', 'if you believed . . . do not believe . . .'), appropriate for the moment when Jesus spoke, were still appropriate for John's own time. The Jews' own Scriptures continue to testify to Jesus, the new, the latest, 'Word' expressing God's mind. But it is sadly, and dangerously, easy to become so devoted to the written record of what God said centuries ago as to become deaf to anything God is saying in one's own time.

Suggestions for group discussion:

1   Reading over 5:41–44, let the group consider what light these verses throw upon the cult of self-promotion that makes up so much modern Church and evangelistic advertising. Is that a fair application of Christ's thought?

2   Traditional ways of saying that 'God was in Christ', 'Jesus was God

incarnate', 'Jesus the Word God spoke', now puzzle as much as they impress. We have tried 'Christ the vehicle, the channel, of deity', 'the mirror-reflection of God', 'a prism through which deity shone undistorted'. Others offer 'Christ is the strand upon which the ocean of deity washes our shores', 'the human face of God'. Can the group find, or quote, better modern-sounding phrases for the same essential truth? Do they like: 'Christ, a soul tuned in constantly upon God's wavelength'; 'God's rear stair-way into the souls of men'; 'a visitor from beyond Mars'?

Jesus—true manna from heaven   *John 6:1–71*

Back in Galilee, miracle yet again leads to contention. To the miraculous picnic in the other three Gospels, John adds significant and provocative details, on several levels of meaning simultaneously. One outcome of the resulting conflict is the loss of many disciples, and the close (in John's account) of Christ's ministry in Galilee, except for the very brief summary in 7:1.

John alone mentions the boy with the barley loaves and cured fish, a typical peasant meal. He makes the initiative Christ's, not the disciples', and introduces the crucial reaction of the crowd (15), and the synagogue sermon and argument next day. In consequence, John gives very much more space to the story, and far greater importance, than do the other evangelists.

Jesus questions Philip (5) presumably as knowing the district well. Does John mean that Jesus tested his initiative, or his faith? or simply that Jesus did not need to seek information? It was Jewish polite custom to leave fragments, after a banquet, for the servers—here, a basketful each! The movement of the ships is obscure; compare 17 with Mark 6:45. Capernaum and Bethsaida being barely five miles (8km) apart, the general direction could be described either way. 'Across the sea' probably means along the coast from headland to headland, waiting to pick up Jesus as he came down from the hills.

Jesus' 'walking on the sea' is linked with this miracle in all accounts, though John does not call it a miracle, and it seems a self-serving wonder. The same expression, 'on the sea' (in Greek, and also in English place-names, 'Southend-on-Sea'), is used for beside the sea at 21:1 (and only slightly differently at 6:21). On the other hand, the disciples' fear, Jesus' reassurance, and the glad relief of 21, do suggest that John had miracle in mind.

Verses 22–24 have become confused; most probably the meaning is 'the people who remained ... had seen that there was only one boat ... and that Jesus had not entered it. However, boats from Tiberias came... So the next day, when the people saw that Jesus was not there... they themselves got into these boats and went... seeking Jesus.'

Jesus brushes aside the irrelevant question in 25 to rebuke the crowd's mercenary motive, and contrast with it a hunger for the food which endures to life eternal. By so doing, Jesus invests the whole event with immense new meanings. The people had seen the miracle but had not seen its point—to John's mind, a vital difference. That point was, the offer of 'eternal food' through Jesus, the Son of man, whom God had authorized. (The reference to Jesus being 'sealed' seems irrelevant here; but the enticing suggestion that the seal alludes to the baker's mark on loaves is not supported by John's language.)

The counsel not to labour for perishable food (echoing Isaiah 55:2) prompts the question in 28, and Jesus' reply evokes the request for a sign on which faith might rest. This may have come from Jews in Capernaum who had not witnessed the previous day's miracle; the final words (31) show that they had heard of it, and disparaged it as 'nothing new'.

The objection voiced in 42 is also brushed aside; Jesus' human origin is unimportant: his ultimate origin is 'from heaven'. It is surprising that John does not provide the full answer for his readers, but he never refers to Christ's birth of a virgin. It is possible that John is being ironical—'If the objectors had only known!' But that implies that he expects his readers to know the answer, although he is writing to instil belief.

In 66–67 we learn that, at least in Galilee, many disciples 'went about' with Jesus, though not of the Twelve. John has not named the inner circle, nor recorded their appointment. Here, too, we learn that 'Iscariot' was the name also of Judas' father (so 13:26), which tends to confirm that it means 'man of Kerioth' (in Judea), rather than containing some allusion to Judas' character.

The story itself, then, is fairly straightforward: the various meanings woven into it are complex and very significant. John alone sets the story in the atmosphere of Passovertime (4–5, 'then'). It seems Jesus did not attend that year, and the present meal acquires the nature of a 'Galilean Passover' for those unable to travel, but without the Passover lamb, though full of memories of the exodus from Egypt (31, 49, 58; 14 likewise echoes words of Moses, Deuteronomy 18:15, 18).

This Passover undertone lends great force to the repeated comparison of Jesus with Moses. Beginning with the echo of Moses in 5 (see Numbers 11:21–22), and the people's comment in 14, the Jesus-or-Moses theme is resumed next day (31) with recall of Moses' greatest miracle, the gift in the wilderness of bread from heaven. This rivalry controls the synagogue discussion.

Jesus corrects the critics' assertion: it was not Moses who gave the manna but God, who still gives the true bread from heaven, that which gives life to the world. As usual, there is literalist misunderstanding, and a request for 'this bread always' (as 4:15). This leads Jesus to the explicit claim that he is the bread of life, come down to satisfy the hunger and thirst of all who believe in him. (Philo, similarly, had spoken of the Word as giving heavenly food for the soul; both Greeks and Jews would understand the metaphor—see 1 Corinthians 10:3; Psalm 78:25; Nehemiah 9:15.)

To this claim the Jews object strongly (41–42), but Jesus repeats it (48), adding that the fathers who ate the manna died, whereas those who eat of the bread from heaven will live for ever. Since he himself is the living bread, the sustenance he gives that the world may live is his flesh. The sharp contrast between himself and Moses, between his ever-living followers and the fathers who died, is repeated in 58. Throughout, Jesus does nothing to soften the comparisons. Of the 'manna' Jesus provided, even the fragments could be preserved, as Moses' manna could not be (Exodus 16:19–20). The manna Jesus offered would give life, not to a few small tribes but to the world (33), and it would confer not temporary survival for a journey, but eternal life. Jews could scarcely be expected to hear such claims without murmuring, disputing, complaining about 'a hard saying', and taking offence (41, 52, 60–61).

So far the debate was about things long ago. A much more urgent issue concerned the possibility that Jesus was Messiah. It was widely believed that at the Babylonian exile the pot of manna preserved within the temple had been hidden, to be recovered by Messiah (see Revelation 2:17). The expected prophet who would be like Moses, about whom the excited crowd murmured, was also popularly associated with Messiah's arrival (14).

The title which Jesus kept using, 'Son of man', though ambiguous, was widely used of the Messiah by apocalyptic writers (see 27, 53, 62); and the fourfold claim to raise the dead (39–40, 44, 54) yet again had messianic overtones. Of all this a Jewish crowd would be acutely aware. Understandable, therefore, and far more dramatic was the startling attempt to 'take Jesus by force' (a strong phrase, meaning 'lay hands upon', 'snatch', 'kidnap' as at 10:12, 28–29) and crown him king, there and then (15).

Jesus' immediate and decisive reaction confirms that this marked a dangerous crisis. He '*made* the disciples to get into the boat . . . while he *dismissed* the crowd' and himself disappeared 'into the hills to pray' (so Mark 6:45–46; the Greek words are emphatic). Each detail is assumed by John; 15, 16–21, 24 imply that the crowd had been sent away first. The strategy is clear, to get away himself, alone, while also separating the disciples from the crowd, neither of whom could he completely trust at such a moment. Some early copies say that Jesus 'fled' to the hills, a reading which could well be original.

Did the old temptation recur even to Jesus himself, to win a crown by feeding the crowds (Matthew 4:1–4)? Plainly, such an attempt to proclaim Jesus king could destroy all his work, contradict his teaching, and endanger his life. The incident reveals the simmering nationalism and violence in the midst of which Jesus' ministry was conducted (compare Mark 15:7). In this light, the meal on the hillside, for minds looking for a signal (or an excuse), might assume the appearance of a messianic banquet—and start a report sufficient to initiate a rebellion.

However, John has still not finished his exposition of this picnic. Astonishingly, beyond the miracle, the Passover atmosphere, the rivalry with Moses, the true manna, and the messianic implications, John brings us to the inner meaning of the Lord's Supper! This must be later reflection developing the story; neither Jews nor disciples could have grasped such an idea in the synagogue at Capernaum before Jesus died. Bread for the hungry (27, 32–35) becomes Jesus' flesh (51) to be eaten, along with the drinking of his blood, if any are to have life or see resurrection (53–54). His flesh is food indeed, his blood drink indeed; and as Christ lives because of the Father, so he who eats Christ will live because of him. Such eating ensures mutual indwelling (55–57).

No Christian reader, in John's time or since, could miss the allusion here to the sacrament of bread and wine. The Greek word for 'giving thanks' in 11, 23, has given to the Christian Communion service one of its most widely-used names, 'the eucharist'; and as soon as the Church began to decorate her places of worship, the five loaves and two fishes of this story were represented upon the Lord's Table. Certainly no blood was drunk, or symbolized, at the meal in Galilee; the very thought would be abhorrent to every Jewish mind.

Yet John has, by implication, rooted the most characteristic act of Christian worship in the life-history of Jesus, and extended the feeding of five thousand in Galilee to every Lord's Table and altar in Christendom. And what Jesus meant by giving his flesh for the life of the world (51) could only be understood many months afterwards, as Christians reflected upon the death and resurrection of the Saviour of the world. (Verses 54, 56–58, are all in the present continuous tense, stretching through Christian history. John knew that the 'offence' mentioned in 61, also, persisted into his own time.)

Alongside these allusions, metaphors, and symbolisms, John mean-while states his meaning in simple, evangelical terms. Jesus feeds the mind, heart, and spirit, of each one who believes in him, imparting and nourishing an eternal life that will be crowned with immortality. This gift is available to those who 'come' (35, 37, 44, 65), who 'see' (36, 40, 62), and who 'believe' (eight times). The initiative remains with God, in 'drawing' souls and 'giving' them to Jesus (44, 65, 37, 39). Jews used the terms 'drawing', 'bringing' of making proselytes; the metaphor was taken from net-fishing (see 21:6; 12:32).

Yet the reception of such an experience depends upon 'doing the work' of continually believing in Jesus, hearing and learning from the Father, being taught by God, receiving and assimilating Christ as one receives and assimilates food (29, 35, 54–58). In 46 John again guards against the claim that any one but Jesus has ever had direct 'mystical' knowledge of God, or could come to the Father but by him (so 1:18; 14:6).

Nothing hinders any soul's so coming, seeing, believing, except its own attitude and resistance. It is the will of the Father that everyone who sees and believes shall have eternal life, and it is the will of the Son to cast out no one who comes to him (40, 37). The teaching is for all; Christ's flesh is given for the life of the world (45, 51).

These are the words which prove to be 'spirit and life' to those who believe (63). We meet again the contrast between spirit and flesh. It is the spirit only which can give life; the flesh, whether physical manna, common food, or sacramental elements, religion, legal morality, or human philosophy, can achieve nothing eternal, as Jesus told Nicodemus.

And the same spiritual, life-imparting words distinguish those who believe from those who betray (64). Jesus' insight into human nature is emphasized once more (61, 64). But if the hard saying about eating Christ's flesh and drinking his blood made some followers stumble, there would be yet more wonderful truths still to be grasped—Christ's resurrection and ascension, for example (62; compare 1:51). Faith must brace itself to keep up with Jesus!

So John's description of Jesus' ministry in Galilee closes with sharp division between those who go away and those who have no one else to go to. Spoiled for their former lifestyle, they are unfitted to return to where Christ found them. They hunger, now, for words of eternal life. They have believed (the first step), and come to know by experience (the second step) that Jesus is the Holy One of God (68–69). As in Mark 8:29, it is Peter who voices on behalf of others ('we') the essence of the Christian confession. Sadly, Jesus remarks that that is not true of them all (with 70 compare 13:2). In the light of all that had just happened and been said, Judas' attitude seemed to require more than human wickedness to explain it.

81

Another magnificent chapter! Such an unfolding of meaning within meaning in meditation upon a simple story leaves no possible doubt of John's greatness, and acuteness, of mind. Or of his deep spiritual insight.

Suggestions for group discussion:

1   In the light of 6:53–58, do we modern Christians make enough of the euch-arist or Communion service? Some churches read part of this chapter at each celebration, other churches never do—perhaps nervous of its implications. What does the group think?

2   The crisis described in 6:15, and Christ's strong reaction to it, illustrate the dangerous atmosphere of 'simmering nationalism and violence' in which Jesus ministered. Has this anything to teach us about the alliance of Christianity with 'liberation movements' in various parts of the modern world?

Jesus attends the feast   *John 7:1–31*

Without giving details, John records that Jesus continued to tour Galilee, to avoid the death threat to which 5:18 refers. But the issue between Jesus and the Jewish authorities could not long be evaded. The imminence of the Feast of Tabernacles, and unexpected pressure from Jesus' brethren, brought matters to a head. Jesus himself was evidently considering whether his time had come (6, 8, 30).

From earliest times some copyists thought that the 'contradiction' between 8 and 10 required correction and boldly inserted 'yet' in 8. In view of the danger (even in Galilee, 6:15), the brothers' argument has been thought foolish, or ironical, even mocking. It might however have been provoked by Jesus' loss of popularity (6:66)—assuming they would regret that. Stranger still is Jesus' hesitant response. There can have been no intention to deceive (John would never suggest that). It has been said that Jesus would never allow others to influence his action, but would obey God only. Yet a pagan official, a Syrophoenician mother, the faith of a sick man's four friends, the great faith of a centurion, were all allowed to convey God's will to him.

Was Jesus then merely hesitating, awaiting the Father's clear direction? His ministry had begun with forty days reviewing, alone, the various ways in which a kingdom could be won. Before choosing the Twelve, Jesus spent a night alone in prayer. In Gethsemane, some idea of what was still 'possible', as alternative to death, could still briefly occupy his mind. John does emphasize the humanity of Jesus: is he not in 2–10 showing us again the depth of Jesus' dependence on the Father's will as he hesitates, considers the probabilities, waits for guidance, before committing himself to what might prove (and did prove) an irrevocable step?

Such consideration was necessary. Jesus' brothers urged a public appearance, with boldness (3–4, Greek), and it was this which Jesus declined. The essence of his reply was 'You can go any time . . . Yours is a private visit . . . The world does not hate you, you are in no danger . . . It is not so with me . . .' Verse 10 makes this clear; the consequences show how right Jesus was to hesitate.

Arriving late and unnoticed, Jesus found the city of Jerusalem buzzing with excited rumours—Would Jesus come? Would they see him this time?—and eager, though secret arguments about who he was. The atmosphere was highly charged, and with his usual dramatic timing Jesus stepped into the midst of the suppressed discussion by appearing in the temple, teaching (11–14).

In this way Jesus was protected by the presence, and the divisions, of the festival crowds. The inactivity of the authorities (25–26), and the failure of the officers to arrest him when action was belatedly attempted (32, 45–46), only increased the confusion and fed the muttered conjectures of the people. Jerusalem became a fertile scene for public discussion, and the feast an opportune moment for public decision, on the great questions confronting Jewry: What authority had this man of Nazareth? Is not this the one the authorities sought to kill, yet they seem unready! Would even Messiah do more miracles than he does? When he says he will be going away, what does he mean (11–12, 25–26, 31, 34–36)?

Debate continued for three days, from the middle of the feast to the eve of the last day (14–31). The wisdom and eloquence of Jesus surprised and disconcerted his hearers; Rabbis gave much study to the art of public disputation, but Jesus was technically untrained, a 'lay' man (15). Jesus replied that his authority did not rest upon training, but upon his divine mission (16); perceiving his authority, therefore, is not a question of official status, but of readiness to hear and obey God. The selfless motive of the teacher is the best guarantee of his sincerity (17–18). But speaking of authority, Jesus asks was not Moses the Jews' boasted authority? Then why did they not keep Moses' Law, instead of seeking to kill him, which was against the Law? The people dismiss this as some demonic persecution mania. Jesus recalls the attempted assassination on his last visit to Jerusalem (5:16–18).

Jesus adds a new argument in defence of that sabbath healing: if the part-surgery of circumcision was officially allowable on the sabbath, why was the cure of the whole man on the sabbath held to be unlawful? Their moral judgments were superficial, and confused (22–24). Some have felt that this recalling of a five-months-old miracle is strange, and propose to transfer 19–24 to the close of chapter 5. This is plausible. But three days of argument would have rehearsed all that Jesus had said and done on his previous visit. Besides, for John's readers, chapters 5 and 7 were separated not by five months but by a few turns of the scroll.

The suspicion among the crowd that the authorities are afraid to kill Jesus, because secretly they know him to be Messiah, is very life-like. Many believed the origin of Messiah a divine secret; or that he would appear at Bethlehem; or on the clouds; or suddenly from obscurity (27). To these speculations Jesus replies with an ironical question (28). The real issue, however, lies deeper: the true origin of Jesus is the Father. For all their pride in religion, the Jews did not know God! Jesus knew him, came from him, was on his mission (28–29).

Such a charge was especially sharp when laid against God's chosen people. Inevitably, some clamoured for Jesus' arrest, to silence him. But the hour for that had not yet come. Others—'many'—believed in him, being unable to imagine a more impressive Messiah.

Hesitations over, Jesus had certainly arrived, publicly, where the action was, and manifested himself, clearly and contentiously, in a way the city authorities could not ignore.

Suggestions for group discussion:

1 In religious affairs, the nature, source and ground of spiritual authority is always a contentious question. Does it lie in the office a person holds? In the personality holding the office? In training and experience? In the things a person actually says (as sermons), or does (as sacraments)—whoever says or does them? Or only in worthy sayers and doers? In the Church as a whole? What light does 7:15–18 throw upon such questions?
2 Is public contention about religious questions, in press or broadcasting or on platforms, a good or bad thing, helpful to the religious cause or better avoided? Would silence, apathy, or ignoring such subjects be an advantage?

Three daring claims   *John 7:32—8:59*

When certain Pharisees had reported the crowd's excited mutterings about Jesus to the authorities, steps were at last taken to silence him (recall 25–26). The appearance of arresting officers would immediately heighten tension, even if Jesus had not himself perceived its meaning and announced the imminent end of his ministry, and of the people's opportunity. Very soon now, *they* would be seeking *him*, but would not find him.

There is irony in the speculation that Jesus intends to carry his ministry to the somewhat despised Jews living among Gentiles beyond Palestine (35). John and his readers well know that this turning to the Gentiles had in fact occurred, with immense success.

At this heated and crucial moment, at the climax of the great festival, with the swollen crowds arguing about him, the authorities ordering his arrest, the temple police waiting their opportunity but intimidated by the crowd's mood, Jesus chose to issue three tremendous claims. Each was calculated to shock the city. Each dared anyone to touch him.

The Feast of Tabernacles celebrated the harvest ingathering, and perpetuated the ancient nomadic traditions from which so much that was pure and prophetic in Judaism had sprung. The holiday was spent in 'tents' of leafy branches, recalling Israel's wilderness journeying, and great incidents of that journey were solemnly re-enacted (Leviticus 23:33–36; Deuteronomy 16:13).

On each of the feast's seven days, priests in ceremonious procession carried a golden flask, filled at the pool of Siloam, to the temple to be outpoured as a libation of thanksgiving for the water that had gushed from the rock at the touch of Moses' rod (Exodus 17:6; Psalm 105:41). The story was read, thanksgiving was offered for the rains and streams that had made another harvest possible, and prayers were offered for the 'latter rain' that would soften the parched ground for re-ploughing.

It was a dignified and impressive service, until, on the last, 'great' day of the series Jesus chose his moment to shout across the hushed temple courtyard, over the heads of the reverent crowd—'If any one thirst, let him come to *me...*' And into the outraged silence added the resounding promise: 'He who believes in me... "out of his heart shall flow rivers of living water" '! We can scarcely imagine the effect.

Among the Scriptures read, chanted or recited in the water-ritual was the promise of Zechariah (14:8) that living waters shall flow out of Jerusalem (which Rabbis had called the navel of the world). Jesus echoes Zechariah closely, but substitutes the Christian believer for the city. John interprets with hindsight: Jesus spoke of the Spirit, not given until Jesus departed (so 16:7). Rabbis had already forged a link between the water outpoured at Tabernacles and the prophecies concerning the giving of the Spirit. All in all, the authorities could hardly complain of Jesus' language and allusions, but his claim... (37–39)!

As with the gift of true manna, a deliberate comparison with Moses is implied by Jesus' provocative act, and the Christian fulfilment of what Jewish ritual could only foreshadow. So bold a declaration, so massive a claim, convinced some that only the long-awaited prophet dare speak so; and others, that only Messiah himself could so act (40–41). Yet the difficulty of Jesus' supposed birthplace remained to puzzle some (as the failure of John to clear up their ignorance, even for his readers, remains to puzzle us). Still others, affronted by Jesus' interruption of the sacred ritual, sought his immediate arrest, but feared to touch him (42–44).

How Jesus so dared, John then explains. Behind the public scene the arresting officers returned to the priests and Pharisees reporting the power of Jesus' eloquence—and they were men accustomed to listening to interminable religious talk! The authorities' arrogant reply expresses again the pride that closed Jewish minds against Jesus (47–49). In sharp contrast, the plea of Nicodemus for a fair hearing for Jesus was an act of great courage.

Yet again Jesus' supposed Galilean origin is held to be sufficient refutation of his claims. Christian readers would know that northern Israel had produced its prophets, and that Jesus was born at Bethlehem, while even readers not yet Christian could see for themselves how irrelevant the argument was. Jesus' claim, to refresh and perpetually renew every thirsty soul, and two or three generations of believers to testify to its truth, still remained to confront a world spiritually exhausted. No quibble about origins could deny that.

For commentary on John 7:53—8:11, see the next subsection.

As night fell, the Tabernacle ritual changed. Now it re-enacted with equal dramatic force the story of the pillar of fire and cloud that led Israel through the wilderness (Exodus 13:21–22). In the temple's 'court of women' the great golden candelabrum was lit; every courtyard in Jerusalem had its bonfire; dancing, singing processions with flaring torches encircled the city, praising God for the gift of light at creation, in the desert, and at every dawn. While the rulers still argued, Jesus appeared again among the seething crowds and made his second great claim ring across the brightly-lit scene—'I am the world's pillar of fire; he who follows me need never wander more; he will possess the light of life' (so 8:12 implies).

To Jewish ears such a claim constituted near-blasphemy; the Lord himself was Jewry's light, and the Law her all-sufficient daily guide. But John is aware that light figured as largely in the worship of Mithras, of Hermes, and in Persian and Egyptian worship of the sun. John rarely forgets his mixed readership.

The Pharisees chose again to rebut Christ's claim as self-testimony, unacceptable in Jewish Law. This time Jesus denies the principle: self-testimony can be true, especially when (like the prophets of old) the speaker comes from God. The Pharisees' judgment is 'fleshly' and false, because they do not understand that Jesus' authority derives from his divine mission. His testimony is not self-serving, but involved in his service of God. What is more, their statement is untrue: for Jesus has the corroborative testimony which the Law requires—the Father himself bears witness to him (8:13–18; see commentary on 5:31–40).

The critics' demand, 'Where is your Father?', was the correct legal reply, for appeal to a witness who could not be produced in court was forbidden. But Jesus turned the clever question back upon the Jews, as an admission that they did not know the Father! Such an audacious charge against the highest religious authorities in the land seems to have silenced them for a time. Those who challenged Jesus to argument never came off best.

Turning from the hecklers to the crowd, Jesus reiterates the warning that the city has not long to make up its mind. Opposition is growing sharper, and bolder. Soon he will be no longer among them; rejecting the salvation he offers, they must die in their sins. So they will not come where he is going. When, misunderstanding his meaning, the people begin to speculate on intended suicide, Jesus underlines the truth that he and they are worlds apart (21–23).

With these words, the issue is set before each hearer (and reader) in its clearest form: either believe, or die unsaved. The belief required is also defined: 'that I am' ('that I am the one I claim to be' is the NIV paraphrase; 'that I am what I am' is the NEB paraphrase; the Greek means simply 'I am'; see on 4:26). This utterance, like 4:26, may be thought one of the occurrences of 'I am' that catch 'the accent of deity' (24).

Such a statement inevitably evoked further indignant protest— 'Who do you think you are?' Jesus' reply is, unfortunately, very obscure. RSV, NEB, NIV all offer 'What I have been claiming all along', which sounds like a dismissive end to discussion. Because ancient copies differ considerably, RSV, NEB also offer 'Why do I' (or 'should I') 'talk to you at all?', which suggests a loss of patience. The following verses support the former interpretation.

Jesus then declares that there is much more he could say, but forbears, in obedience to him who sent him; this again is misunderstood (26–27). Jesus comments that they will not understand until his death and resurrection make all plain. 'Lifted up' was so used at 3:15 (see comment). It means the one act of death-resurrection-ascension that would vindicate Christ's claims and demonstrate the Father's complete approval of his ministry. Meanwhile Jesus lived and served with the constant sense of the Father's presence and the Father's pleasure (28– 29). But Jesus' ambiguous phrase carried also an implication of death by crucifixion. This solemn change of tone evidently persuaded many that Jesus was sincere, and perhaps also of their own responsibility. These believed in him, at least to the point of taking his side (the Greek words may suggest incipient faith only; note 31–33).

At this point one might expect—might even hope!—that the crowd would disperse, and the long argument evaporate in muttered discontent. But it was the last night of the holiday, to be dragged out as long as possible. Morning would bring separation, the long journey to distant villages, the resumption of routine. And with nothing settled about Jesus! Religious discussion with any available Rabbi was a feature of Jewish social life, and a means of entertainment. Besides, Jesus' reassuring promise to those who had just begun to believe (32) was provocative enough to start further debate.

For Jesus said that provided they continued in his teaching the truth would vindicate itself to them, and they would know the freedom truth always confers. Evidently this was overheard by bystanders less friendly (40, 44–45, 48, 52, 59). The question in 33 may be a simple request for explanation, somewhat naïve in view of Israel's bondage to other peoples, from Egypt to Rome. Perhaps their fierce assertion of moral and religious freedom against every oppressor was in their minds.

The answer of Jesus, here very condensed, focuses upon this inner spiritual freedom which loyalty to truth achieves, freedom from the power of falsehood and sin, freedom from fear, and from exposure. The Jews may boast of descent from Abraham (33, 37, 38), but Abraham had two sons. Ishmael, a child of slavery, was banished; only Isaac inherited Abraham's promise and privilege. Which of the two kinds of 'descendant of Abraham' (slave-born or free) any particular Jew is, only his conduct will show (39). Those who sin reveal their slavery thereby (34); those now plotting to kill him because he spoke God's word, are not doing as Abraham did, and are therefore not true sons (37–40). (This distinction between true and false descendants of Abraham had become the main argument of Christians against the Jewish doctrine of exclusive divine election: compare Romans 2:28–29; 9:6–8; Philippians 3:3; Matthew 3:9).

Only the true son of Abraham, one never to be banished, can bequeath true freedom (36). Those whose conduct is so unlike Abraham's show that they have another father altogether (38–40). This harsh charge evoked yet stronger protest, and the higher claim to be children of God himself. Jesus easily counters this (41–42).

The contention grows still sharper: the critics do not understand because they cannot stand the truth. So their true descent, from the father of lies, is revealed. Their plots to kill Jesus confirm this, for the devil was ever a murderer. Having such a lineage, of course they do not believe one who speaks only truth (43–45).

Argument has run into impasse: it is time for decision. They must either convict Jesus of sin or accept the truth he offers. Each man's decision will reveal his character; those who are of God will hear, while those who will not hear are simply not of God (46–47; compare 5:37–42).

To avoid decision, argument takes refuge in abuse. Jesus is a heretic, and a man possessed (for 'Samaritan' see introductory paragraphs, 'For Whom Did John Write', and compare 7:20). It is curious that 'Samaritan' can be mispronounced to sound like 'child of Satan'—a relevant retort after 44. Jesus replies that God will vindicate him in face of such insult, and he repeats the promise of immortality to those who keep his word—a veiled warning to those who do not (48–51)?

Exasperated, the hecklers take this claim as proof of madness (of megalomania as we would say). Abraham was dead, so were the great prophets, yet Jesus' followers will never die! A man must be mad, to claim to be greater than Abraham, than the illustrious prophets! Jesus repeats that he is not claiming glory for himself, that the Father will vindicate him. Though they claim that he is their God too, yet they do not know him. Jesus does know God: that remained, even in John's day, the fundamental issue between Jesus and Judaism—the true conception of God (48–55).

As for descent from Abraham, Jesus reminds his hearers that the Rabbis held that Abraham knew the future, and that the patriarchs would rise to meet Messiah (compare Hebrews 11:8–13). The Jews then ridicule the idea that Jesus could have seen Abraham (so RSV, NEB, NIV), or that Abraham could have seen Jesus (RSV and NEB margins). They declare that he was not yet fifty! (Did Jesus already look near that age?) Jesus responded with perhaps the most provocative, contentious assertion of that momentous day: he said (literally) 'Before Abraham came into existence, I am!' (56–58; compare 1:1; and on 'I am . . .' see commentary on 4:26; 8:24).

At that, abuse turned to violence, attempted stoning for blasphemy. But Jesus eluded them, and the long, crucial day ended. Of course, the whole discussion took less time than it took to record, or takes to unfold; but between ritual, interruption, and argument, the wish of Jesus' brothers had certainly been fulfilled. Jesus had shown himself to the world (59; 7:4).

Jesus' claim to be, for all who would believe, the source of perpetual spiritual refreshment, and the light by which to live from day to day, has obvious significance for all generations. But the claim to antedate Abraham has rather the air of a debating point, or (at first sight) a defiant parting shot intended to silence rather than to convince. The pre-existence of 'the Word' with God had already been affirmed (1:1, 18), and this third daring claim might be seen as at least a necessary consequence of that truth. But something more was implied.

Christianity, in John's day, could still be represented, especially by Jews, as a novel, upstart religion, new-fangled, untried, and ephemeral, as compared with Judaism with its appeal to a centuries-old revelation, the long established Law of Moses, and the unbroken continuity of a chosen people to witness to it. So too, serious Greeks, despite their endless curiosity, and what Luke called (criticizing the Athenians) their tendency to spend their time 'in nothing except telling or hearing something new', valued far more the well-tried teachings of past great thinkers than the multitude of novel philosophies, religions and cults that continually erupted from the East.

For these reasons, Christian apologists appealed constantly to the ancient Scriptures, to the Law and the prophets (1:45), to Moses' foreshadowing of Christ (5:46), in support of 'the mystery hidden for ages and generations' (Colossians 1:26; Ephesians 3:9), and the 'eternal purpose' of God (Ephesians 3:11). Later, men like Clement of Alexandria would claim that Greek philosophy also was a school-master to bring men to Christ, and seek foregleams and preparation for Christian truth in the finer insights of Greek thinkers.

In this broader sense, Christ's third claim may be understood as a declaration that Christ and all he stood for was by no means 'a thing of yesterday', but the ultimate truth enshrined in all creation and history from the first, but only clearly heard when 'the Word became flesh and dwelt among us' (1:1–5, 14).

So the three tremendous claims that enlivened the Feast of Tabernacles all turned upon the central question: whence and who was Jesus? The ultimate reply grew gradually clearer as John's argument proceeded: If you truly knew God, you would recognize Jesus (just as if men truly know Jesus they will see the Father, 14:7, 9). That was in Jesus' day, in John's day, and remains in ours, the final answer to this crucial question. Either we realize that Jesus' claims are true, by spiritual intuition and divine enlightenment, perceiving and welcoming truth by its own light, or we can never be persuaded. To those who venture to believe, truth brings its own vindication in Christian experience.

Suggestions for group discussion:

1 The claims made for or by Jesus in this long passage are among the greatest in the New Testament—source of perpetual refreshment, light of life, link with eternity. Does the group think that the average Christian today thinks in these high terms about the master? Should he?

2 How far would the group judge that modern Christian experience measures up to these claims of Jesus?

A fascinating fragment   *John 7:53—8:11*

As most modern translations show, this paragraph raises exceptional doubts as to its origin, and its proper place in the New Testament—but not, for most Christian minds, as to its truth. A number of manuscript copies of the Gospels, too many and too ancient to ignore, along with early translations and commentaries, do not have these verses. Among those that have the passage, a number mark it as doubtful, or as an insertion; others place it after 7:36, or 7:44, or near the end of John's Gospel, and about twelve have it at Luke 21:38. Where it is present, the paragraph also varies noticeably in detail.

There is obvious need to treat it with some caution. In addition, Greek scholars report that its vocabulary and style are largely unlike John's, some would say more like Luke's. Commentators usually feel that the passage is at least out of place following 7:52; it interrupts the story, adds nothing to the argument, and leaves smoother reading when omitted.

For all that, it is a precious passage, affording an unforgettable glimpse of Jesus, which many defend as a true and early fragment of the oral tradition that circulated in the Church before the Gospels were written. If it ever belonged to John's or Luke's Gospel, it may have been omitted (at first, only from public reading) because it might give the impression that Jesus, and the Church, thought lightly of adultery. But any gospel of divine forgiveness is open to the charge of lightly excusing evil. And here (11) the warning as to future behaviour is as clear as the forgiveness. So the passage is retained, though no one (not even editors of modern versions) really knows where to put it.

Verse 6 is intriguing. It can be understood as expressing Jesus' embarrassment; or his studied refusal to judge; or his 'scribbling impatiently', or just 'doodling' (the word used often means 'drawing'). But the word was also a technical term for writing out an accusation. This gave rise to the suggestion that Jesus was writing a list of the sins society made much fuss about while ignoring far greater evils: writing them therefore in the dust, to express his scorn of popular moral prejudices. A neat guess!

The intention of the accusers was not to kill the woman; the death penalty was no longer within Jewish jurisdiction, and any sentence only rarely ratified by Rome. Their intention was to entrap Jesus into direct public contradiction either of Moses' Law or of Roman law, so giving ground for serious charges. Jesus in reply cites Deuteronomy 17:7, to which the traditional oral law (later recorded in the Mishnah) added the 'hedge' that the accusers themselves must be innocent. That the oldest accusers left first may convey intentional irony: the longer a man lives, the more numerous his accumulated sins.

The woman waited quietly before Jesus, and never was waiting more meaningful or silence more eloquent. Jesus, the only person in the story qualified to condemn, refused to blame. He evidently believed the accusation but knew also the motives of her accusers. His words were wonderfully gentle. He used the same form of address as to his mother (2:4; 19:26). Nevertheless, both parts of the final sentence are equally authoritative. Together they constitute the heart of the Christian idea of forgiveness: full and free pardon without for a moment excusing or condoning wrong.

Seeing and not seeing *John 9:1–41*

This chapter scorns explanation. One feels that John enjoyed writing it as much we do hearing it well read. The place is Jerusalem (7), the time before the Feast of Dedication (three months after the Feast of Tabernacles (10:21–22). The place of the story in the Gospel is due to the illustration it provides of Christ's claim to be the light of the world (8:12). Moreover, the story leads on to the claim to be sole keeper of God's fold. Both functions were also claimed by Judaism; self-manifestation in conflict therefore continues.

Blindness from birth was thought to be incurable (32), which heightens the miracle. Ill-health, affliction, suffering of all kinds, were usually 'explained' either religiously, as punishment for sin (34); superstitiously, as the invasion into personality of some of the millions of creatures, invisible, malignant, swarming in the air, called (not germs! but) 'demons'; or combining superstition with morals, as the work of demons whose invasion was facilitated by sin.

Congenital blindness did not fit into either view very neatly, so the disciples put to Jesus a rabbinic theory that parental sins were visited upon the unborn, especially sin (such as idolatry) committed during pregnancy. Jesus brushes the question aside once more, denying for all time any necessary connection between suffering and sin. He was no theorist. Judaism argued endlessly about suffering, Jesus cured it. RSV, NIV, NEB all understand that this man was born blind 'so that' the work and power of God in Jesus might be shown through him. That idea does not sit easily in Christian minds. But the attempt to re-punctuate the words, as 'not this man ... or his parents. But that the work of God might be manifest in him, we must work ...', though more attractive, has not received the support of Greek scholars. Beside, Jesus repeats the thought at 11:4.

Jesus again speaks of having only limited time (as 7:33; 8:21). His sense of mission gained increasing urgency as Jewish hostility intensified. 'As long as I am in the world...' (5) is full of foreboding.

The traditional means of healing, a saliva salve, would greatly aid a blind man's faith, but the delay is unusual. The journey through the city, with face plastered in clay, to wash at Siloam pool, made the event a public demonstration, and set the city arguing once more about Jesus. Jews would recall similar public acted messages by which prophets like Jeremiah and Ezekiel demanded attention.

John's 'explanation' that 'Siloam' means 'Sent' itself lacks explanation. It seems merely to point a coincidence. That this was the pool from which the water-libation at the Feast of Tabernacles was drawn, linking the miracle with the pillar of fire that lightened Israel's darkness in the wilderness, seems a remote allusion, though Jewish minds were familiar with such linked thoughts. The patient's testimony, 'I went, and washed, and received my sight' (11) later lent warrant to Justin Martyr's description of baptism as 'illumination', and to the early Church's practice of decorating baptismal pools with this scene.

So Jesus brings light to the blind and beggarly (8) life of men: the man's testimony is irrefutable, though (as in John's day) that Christian testimony was contested. The following verses are among the most memorable, and certainly the most amusing, in the Gospel. The authorities' attempts to evade plain evidence, to deny that the man had ever been blind, to involve the man's parents under threat that any who defended Jesus would be cast out of the synagogue; the renewal of the old charge of sabbath-breaking, all are met with the tenacious, pert, almost impertinent counter-arguments of the man who was healed, who will not concede one inch from the experienced facts. Eloquent, unanswerable, and highly entertaining! ('Give God the praise'—verse 24—was a legal formula of oath; compare Joshua 7:19.)

In the end, the defeated Jews resorted again to the bullying assertion of authority, and banished the man from the synagogue. The weight of this punishment depended upon the person punished. It involved social ostracism, possibly unemployment, denial of national status, and probably (later, certainly) exclusion from services of worship and prayer. For the more fearful and superstitious it implied also abandonment to demon forces without divine protection. Usually, such 'casting out' lasted thirty days, or, when formally imposed by the Sanhedrin, until repentance and official forgiveness. In the present instance, a less formal, more localized banishment seems probable. This aspect of the story, and what followed from it (chapter 10), would have special significance for Jewish Christians formally excluded from synagogues about AD85.

Jesus casts no one out (6:37). Instead he seeks out men (35; 1:43; 5:14), in the present case to complete the man's enlightenment and to comfort his wounded spirit (35–38). In 11, Jesus is 'the man called Jesus'; in 17 'a prophet'; in 33 'from God' and not a sinner; in 36 'the Son of Man' (the man knows the title, but seems uncertain if it means Jesus); in 38 he is 'Lord', to be believed and worshipped. So very gradually do some souls come to the faith John is arguing for.

Both Jesus and John summarize the story in 39, perhaps with Isaiah 6:9–10 in mind. The distinction between seeing and perceiving is wholly characteristic of John. Light, in the external world or breaking upon opened eyes, automatically exposes: the coming of Jesus was the judgment of the world because the effect of moral and religious 'light' is to expose the blindness of unbelief (39, compare 3:19–21).

The blind man repeatedly confessed ignorance (12, 25, 36), yet he saw clearly that Jesus is Lord; the Jews constantly asserted their knowledge (16, 22, 24, 29), and they 'saw' the miracle, but they remained blind to its significance. In this sense, by the light of Christ the blind see, and those who think they see better than others are shown to be blind.

Some Pharisees, overhearing, exclaim, 'Are we also blind?' Jesus replies that those who have never seen carry no guilt for not seeing; there is a blindness which is mere ignorance, and is innocent. But those who think they see, claim to see better, and assume they have nothing to learn, are judged by their own boasting, and their guilt remains (41).

Such a charge was especially painful to Pharisees, whose whole position in society, status in religion, and pride of life, rested on their claim to see God's ways and walk meticulously in them. So the issue of rival authorities is raised yet again, but this time in a new form: Who dares to exclude any man from the fold of God, as they had done? Or to readmit him, as Jesus did? That led John to follow the blind man's story with a full record of the discussion that followed, on good, or faithless, shepherds of God's flock.

Suggestions for group discussion:

1   John 9 poses the serious question: whether the Church has, through history, shown itself to be more enlightened than any one else on the problems that beset the world? And as a corollary, whether individual Christians show more enlightened wisdom in the conduct of their lives than unbelievers do?

2   A peculiar affliction of many religious people who claim to see spiritual things, is the 'blind spot'. Good, sincere Christians faced with certain subjects, situations, people, cannot at all see beyond a given point: drunkenness, homosexuality, girls with green eyes, communists, Tibetans, Jews, Roman Catholics, drug addicts—most of us have some particular abhorrence where all tolerance, patience, fairness, impartiality,

desert us. Can the group explain these 'blind spots'—and their cure?

The faithful shepherd   *John 10:1–42*

The official exclusion of the once-blind man from the synagogue, and Jesus' seeking him out to reassure him, obviously raised again the question of who possessed the authority to take such actions. Jesus replies with two metaphors. The background of each is a large common sheepfold, such as modern travellers still describe, an unroofed enclosure usually of stone, with dried thorn-brambles serving as barbed wire along the wall-top. In such a shelter, several shepherds would fold their sheep overnight, and a gate-keeper would keep watch for them all.

Jesus speaks of himself first as the rightful shepherd, neither secret thief nor brazen raider climbing the wall, but approaching openly by the entrance, recognized by the keeper, and by his own sheep among the crowd. Gathering these, his known voice calling each name, he leads them out to pasture. Just so, as the divinely appointed shepherd of souls, does Jesus find his own, and they, responding to his call, follow him willingly. There is nothing false, surreptitious, or furtive about his approach, nothing of bullying threats about his shepherding (as there were in the Pharisees' treatment of the healed man): true hearts recognize Jesus' inherent care and authority, and follow gladly.

Strangely, Jesus' meaning was not understood (perhaps the audience were all city-folk!). Jesus states the same truth another way: he is the entrance for the sheep (7, 9). All who enter by him find security (unlike those banished from the synagogue's protection), and liberty, to go in and out with free hearts, and rich pasture besides (9). This change of metaphor is not so 'violent' as some suppose. From Arabia and Iran come still descriptions of sheepfolds without doors, whose walls and thorns are difficult to negotiate safely or silently; and of modern shepherds who when asked about the open entrance have replied 'I am the door, I sleep across the threshold.' (So, Dr John Van Ess, *Meet the Arab*; Dr William Miller, U.S. Presbyterian Mission, Iran, January 1960.)

Jesus' thought reverts to the shepherd, who unlike raiding thieves comes not to kill but to preserve life, and to enhance it 'to the full' (10 NIV). This he does, if necessary, at the cost of his own life, proving himself a faithful as well as a 'fine' shepherd. (Jesus' word, 'fine' implies skill and devotion rather than general moral goodness.) Those who guard sheep merely for pay will in danger save their own skins and let wolves ravage the flock; the true shepherd regards them as his own, appreciates their value to himself, is pleased when they recognize him as he knows them. Indeed, Jesus knows his own as the Father knows him and he knows the Father, and in that close relationship he lays down his life for them (10–15).

This shepherding of men is part of Christ's mission, for which therefore he carries God's authority. The flock is God's; and not the lost sheep of the fold of Israel only but others further afield, already Christ's ('I have other sheep . . .'), who also must be gathered, and who likewise will recognize their shepherd's voice (16). 'So there shall be one flock, one shepherd'—an announcement of far-reaching significance to Gentiles, but to Jews a blasphemy against the covenant of Jewish election.

Behind all lay the Father's knowledge of the shepherd (15); he loves the shepherd for his self-sacrificing care of the sheep. He has charged the shepherd to lay down his life for the sheep. So, in free obedience to the Father, and not in surrender to human violence, he will lay down his life, and take it again, that the sheep might live (17–18).

In sum, Jesus, alone, is the divinely appointed shepherd of God's sheep and keeper of God's fold. He has unequalled credentials: his direct and open approach; the recognition and response to him of the sheep; his full provision for their needs; his willing surrender of his life to protect them; the Father's complete trust in him. Thus he claims the right to admit or to exclude from the fold of God, though his mission is to gather in all who will hear his voice. Compared with the faithful shepherd, the Jewish authorities, who set themselves up as ranking 'before' Christ (8), are strangers, sheep-rustlers in status, hirelings in motive, never to be depended upon in danger, exploiting God's flock for their own profit.

So Jesus manifested himself once more, in simple language, that winter's day in Jerusalem. But behind the homely imagery lay whole areas of association, for Jesus' hearers and for John's readers alike. The patriarchs, Moses and David had all been shepherds; Psalm 23, and Isaiah, had claimed the shepherd character for God; Jeremiah, Zechariah, Ezekiel, had used the title for human rulers. Especially relevant here is Ezekiel's elaborate contrast of faithful with unfaithful shepherds, and his promise that God himself would one day shepherd his people (Ezekiel 34). All this would echo in Jewish minds as Jesus spoke in Jerusalem (compare Numbers 27:16–17).

And Gentile readers long afterwards knew the language too. From Homer onwards the title 'shepherd' had been applied to gods, heroes, kings in Greece and in Egypt. Philo, too, used the term, applying it to the Word, 'the shepherd of men'. John still interweaves the interests of his varied readers. And by John's time, the language of 1, 5 and 8 would be seen to apply to all pretended shepherds of men, messianic claimants, pagan 'saviours', gods many and lords many.

It is not surprising that this passage in due time found an important place in Christian thought about the pastoral office, helping along with 21:15–17 to frame the ideal for the Christian ministry. The vision of 'one flock' (16) gained great importance, too, as the Church spread far and wide, and her members from Gentile peoples far outnumbered those from Judaism's fold. (The AV/KJV translation, 'there shall be one *fold* rests upon the sole authority of Jerome's erroneous Latin.)

The immediate reaction to Jesus' claim was the usual division of opinion (19–21). Later, a group accosted Jesus in the temple colonnade, eager to resume discussion and corner Jesus with direct questions. He answers the first (24)—he has by no means kept them guessing. As to who he is, that must be perceived by those with insight to discern it; his words and his deeds speak clearly enough to those disposed to believe. Those not so predisposed, who are not of his flock, do not hear, or follow. Those who do, find eternal life and security. They shall not perish, neither shall raiding brigand, sneak thief or wolves ever snatch them from his hand or his Father's. In this, he and his Father are wholly one (22–30).

At this, Jesus is again threatened with (illegal) lynching, and he challenges his accusers to frame in correct legal form the charge against him, by naming which of his good works deserves his death (31–32)! To their reply (33) Jesus answers with (firstly) a Scripture text, Psalm 82:6, which appears to justify his language. There God himself addresses certain 'to whom the word of God came' as 'gods'. Why then is it blasphemy to call God his Father? or to call himself 'the Son of God'? (Jesus does not repeat their misquotation of his words; 33–36.)

When hecklers quibbled about words it was fair enough to pose word-puzzles in reply. Psalm 82:6 was a familiar conundrum. Comparison with similar passages leaves little doubt that the Psalmist was thinking of a divine 'council' of supernatural beings—see Job 1 for one example. But Rabbis cited this verse to show that obedience to the Law could make one 'divinely immortal'. Jesus is meeting obstinate critics on their own ground with their own weapons.

But (secondly) the issue is too important to leave there. Why should such language, even if scriptural, apply especially to Jesus? Because it is he whom God 'consecrated and sent into the world', as the quality of his works makes plain. If he is not doing God-like things, then by all means let them not believe in him (37). Here again he appeals to their own moral judgment upon his words and deeds: that way, or even if by the deeds alone, they may come eventually to faith (37–38). The discussion has returned upon its beginning (38, compare with 30).

Once more the hearers, baffled in argument, turn to threaten violence. But Jesus 'escaped': for the fifth time since the fateful decision of 7:10 (7:45–46; 8:20, 59; 10:31, 39). This time, Jesus also withdrew from further challenge and contention to the place where John's story began, beyond the Jordan (1:28; 3:22). There Jesus remained, apparently for some three months, until the death of Lazarus and the approach of Passover drew him back to Judea.

But even there many sought him out, and recalling the testimony that the Baptist had borne to him in that place, and how it had been confirmed in Jesus' ministry, they 'believed in him there' (40–42).

It is a real loss that for most readers today the pastoral language of Scriptures like Psalm 23 and John 10 seems remote, sentimental, unreal, romantic. So very few have ever met a working shepherd, have any idea of the shepherd's work, or know one breed of sheep from another. It is essential therefore, if Jesus' meaning is to make its true impact, that we make a real effort of imagination, and think back to the arduous labour day and night, the varying weather, the serious responsibilities (shepherds usually had to pay for each lost sheep), and the dangers, natural and criminal, of the shepherd's life. (Genesis 31:38–40; Jeremiah 25:34–37; 49:19–20; Ezekiel 34:2–4, 6, 12, 16; Amos 3:12; Luke 15:3–6; John 10:11–12 will fill the picture.)

Against that background, the claim to be the faithful shepherd of souls and keeper of God's fold, even at the cost of life itself, takes on new realism and relevance. God has 'brought back from the dead our Lord Jesus, that great Shepherd of the sheep' (Hebrews 13:20 NIV), through whom alone all we who like sheep have gone astray can regain security, find liberty, and enjoy life abundant.

Suggestions for group discussion:

1   Remembering that Jesus alone is the shepherd and the door giving entrance to God's fold, are we right to lay stress upon our conditions for church membership?

2   Do members of the group find in parts of this familiar chapter any particular spiritual comfort precious to themselves? Would they share their feelings, or experience, about it?

Life restored at mortal risk   *John 11:1–54*

Jesus' self-manifestation in conflict reaches its unforgettable climax in the most dramatic of all Jesus' signs, and the most astounding claim that ever passed human lips. Here, too, is John's supreme irony: for the greatest miracle is the restoration of life that so quickly brings about Jesus' death.

This, by John's account, the last magnificent challenge to Jerusalem, is made at the place (Bethany, only two miles away) and the time (as crowds of pilgrims passed through on their way to Passover) of maximum impact. Jesus was still in retreat beyond Jordan (10:40), though his friends knew where to find him, when news arrived of the serious sickness of Lazarus, one of the three dearly loved friends whose hospitality he often shared. It is curious that in introducing these friends, John should anticipate the story of Christ's anointing, which he has still to tell but which he can assume the readers know. The effect is very moving.

Jesus' reactions are strange. He says that Lazarus' illness is 'not unto death', but later, that Lazarus has died (4, 11, 13); the sequel explains that indeed Lazarus has not died finally. By John's time, 'sleep', implying eventual awakening, had become a common Christian term for death. It occurs twelve times in the New Testament, and was known also in Jewish and pagan circles. Jesus' meaning was not immediately clear to the disciples; this time we may sympathize with their misunderstanding.

But Jesus' delay (6) is more puzzling. A day's journey each way plus two days' delay means that Lazarus was dead when (or soon after) the messenger set out, and Jesus seems to have known this (39, 14). It appears that Jesus was waiting for death to be 'certified': the Rabbis taught that the hovering spirit left the body and dissolution began on the fourth day. This lends an air of planning, almost of stage-management, to the miracle.

But John emphasizes that there was no lack of concern, of deep love, on Jesus' part. Nevertheless, Jesus can speak of being glorified by means of Lazarus' death, and of being glad he was not present (to heal?) 'so that you may believe' (4, 15). In verse 9, too, Jesus speaks of walking in daylight, and so not stumbling, as though something dark to him had now become clear. All of which suggests that the death of Lazarus has presented a course of action not possible before, namely to return to Jerusalem at Passover for one last sign and the greatest miracle of all. There may be an impression of deliberate planning involving the deep grief of friends; but it is nearer the truth to speak of an opportunity seized, which would bring the friends great joy and serve his own purposes also.

Yet the situation was full of danger, as the disciples foresaw. Five times Jesus had barely escaped violence in Judea (see commentary on 10:39). Jesus' reply, affirming that a man is safe until his work is done, his 'twelve hours' fulfilled, shows that already he is aware of peril and of limited time. Thomas' loyal despair, a steadfast attachment to Jesus in the midst of bewilderment and danger, has earned him the tribute 'the dogged disciple'. His realism, courage and constancy deserve to be remembered alongside his later doubt—due to realism (8–16; 14:5; 20:24–28).

Verse 19, like the burial cave and the anointing story, indicates that the Bethany home was of some social standing and importance. The active Martha, and reticent, retiring Mary, correspond with Luke's picture of the sisters (Luke 10:38–42). Martha's first words, expressing complete confidence in Jesus and regret at his absence, had evidently passed between the sisters (21 = 32), but Martha adds not a request but an affirmation that God will even yet do whatever Jesus asks. Jesus offers the clear assurance of resurrection, without saying when. Martha replies in slightly credal tone, repeating the belief of the Pharisees, of the 'Eighteen Benedictions' recited daily in the synagogues, and of most of the common people. It clung to hope, but at some distant, utterly remote future (20–24).

Jesus answers with the breathtaking proclamation of 25–26. Martha is standing already in the presence of resurrection! Jesus himself is, here and now, resurrection and life; though a believer in him dies, yet shall he live; whoever lives and believes 'shall never, ever, die'. This last phrase is the literal translation, and significant. Jews considered the body to be necessary to complete personality, and so emphasized resurrection; Greek thought (which John ever keeps in mind) desired only the immortality of the soul, freed from the body in the never-dying life of the spirit. Jesus fulfils both expectations.

According to this one saying, immortality is conditional, depending upon belief, and is essentially the continuation through death of the eternal and abundant life which Jesus gives now, already, to his own (5:24; 10:27–28). With a wider reference, 5:29 speaks as clearly of a resurrection to life and a resurrection (apparently of unbelievers) to judgment.

Jesus asked Martha for a clear, present commitment to this Christian hope. She gives it (27) with a plain, unhesitating 'Yes, Lord', and then adds the sufficient statement of what has been the ground of Christian hope through all succeeding centuries, faith in Christ as Son of God, long promised and now sent into the world.

Such revelation is not to be kept to oneself. Martha immediately invited Mary to meet Jesus, using the title 'Teacher' that disciples seem to have used among themselves. Mary responded at once: John's description reads like a firsthand account. Onlookers assumed that Mary was paying the required daily visit to the tomb. Mary repeated to Jesus the regret so often voiced between the women, but Jesus made no reply, except to join her weeping (28–33).

The watching Jews were deeply impressed by Jesus' gift of sympathy, though some wondered that he had not been present to heal. All, disciples, sisters, onlookers, seem to agree that Jesus loved Lazarus enough, and had the power, to prevent this tragedy. Why had he not come in time (34–37)?

Closely linked with this question, immediately before and immediately after it, John refers to the deep distress of Jesus; certainly Jesus shared the family grief; certainly he felt the weight of human mortality; but John's word in 33 and 38 (the word in Greek suggests 'the snort of an angry horse') is far too strong to express sympathy. Yet anger or indignation, whether 'at death's power', or at the blame imputed to himself, seems in these circumstances totally out of place.

At the least, a deep, shuddering sigh seems intended, perhaps with an added roughness in Jesus' tone as he asked that the stone before the tomb might be removed. At that point, the serious peril attached to what he was about to do must have been vividly present to his mind. Faced with Lazarus' death, the sisters' grief, Jesus knew that he must act for them; faced with the obdurate rejection of the Jewish authorities, he knew that he must challenge them, once again, and for the last time.

He was on the enemies' territory, within their jurisdiction and power to arrest, about to do something they could not possibly ignore. His next words would, in all probability, cost him his own life. And so it happened. He raised Lazarus from death at the price of his own. That is the deadliest irony in the book. And the shuddering sigh before Lazarus' tomb was a momentary anticipation of Gethsemane.

Martha's practical realism speaks again in 39, and with equal bluntness Jesus sets beside the smell of dissolution the glory of God (40). The acknowledgment, yet again, of his total dependence on the Father (41–42) is not a prayer but a thanksgiving for unbroken relationship. The deed about to be done is the Father's work, performed by and through the one the Father sent. His purpose, and his delegated authority, thus made clear once more, anticipating 'the last day' (of 5:21, 25; 6:39–40), Jesus issued the loud summons, magnificent as God's 'Let there be light' at creation, 'Lazarus, come out.'

The climax is beyond comment.

Miracles, in this Gospel, lead always to faith, hostility, or to both. The hostility here is immediate, official, and final (47–53; 12:9–11). Jesus' increasing influence and its dangers are fully acknowledged by John (45–53); the underlying fear is of offending Rome by tolerating a messianic claimant. Caiaphas, in frustration, is singularly rude; 'high priest that year' does not imply annual appointment but 'that fateful, memorable year', or perhaps simply 'at the time'. 'The true priest is always potentially a prophet' Philo said, and John reflects that belief. Though his counsel was cynical and extremely unjust, yet his words came true in ways far beyond his understanding. Believing readers would not miss the point!

The 'other sheep not of this fold' of 10:16 are now (52) 'children of God who are scattered abroad'—'children', perhaps, by virtue of predisposition to receive the gospel (see on 3:19–21). By John's time the Church had witnessed a great 'gathering into one' of these scattered children, as it had witnessed also the total removal by Rome of Jewry's 'holy place and nation'. The alternatives proposed by Caiaphas (50) were both fulfilled.

Caiaphas' advice was accepted, Christ's death resolved upon, and Jesus once again withdrew into obscurity. Nothing is said this time of many seeking him out (10:41–42). The stage is set for tragedy, and Jesus awaits his cue.

The whole story is skilfully written. It is remarkable how death haunts John's account: hinted at, warned, stated, accepted as inevitable, under-lined ('four days'), regretted, consoled, wept over, the tomb, odour, graveclothes... and the theme continues in 50–53, and throughout chapter 12. In face of all this, Judaism could offer only a faint hope of ultimate resurrection, the Sadducees denying even that. In contrast, Jesus offers the immediate, present gift of eternal life. He is himself the representative, the guarantee, and soon to be the embodiment, of the resurrection hope, timelessly alive thereafter. He fulfils already Judaism's meagre creed, spoken by Martha, and the living Lazarus is a prophecy of the rising Christ.

So Judaism is superseded; the whole position of Jewry is endan-gered; and Christianity offers life and immortality to all, at the cost of Jesus' own death. And the generation who read John's book has seen it all happen!

Of course such a story stretches belief. It is of little use to argue the possibility of the Bethany miracle; if Christianity has not supernatural events and possibilities at its heart, including the resurrection of Jesus, the story of Lazarus is not worth discussing. Its absence from Matthew-Mark-Luke is perhaps best explained by the fact that Mark depended mainly on Peter's memories (Matthew and Luke using Mark as one source, also). And there is no sign that Peter was present with Jesus beyond the Jordan or at Bethany; he had a wife and home to care for on occasion, though he rejoined Jesus for the Passover. (This is at least as probable as that he was present and silent! Thomas is spokesman here, 11:16.)

It is true that the other Gospels attribute the decision to kill Jesus to other challenges he offered at that time—the cleansing of the temple, the 'cursing' of the fig tree, the interpretation of Isaiah's parable of the vineyard, the spectacular ride into Jerusalem. If, reflecting on the story long afterwards, John thought that yet another deliberate action of Jesus contributed to the final crisis, why should he be wrong? Few important events spring from single causes, least of all events initiated by Jesus. All in all, the story is far too good to be untrue!

Suggestions for group discussion:

1   Most groups will find more than enough in this passage to explore and take issue with—the explanations offered for Jesus' delay, that anguished, shuddering sigh of Jesus, the difference between the Gospels as to the story, are but examples.

2   In view of the teaching on life hereafter currently offered by certain widespread 'religions' (Spiritualist, Mormon, 'Witnesses' and others), and the barren, heart-breaking sentimentality of secular funeral rites, should the Church be more detailed, clear, and positive about immortality and the hope of resurrection—or be content to admit her ignorance and uncertainty?

Jesus anointed and acclaimed   *John 11:55—12:19*

The stage was set and Jesus at Ephraim awaited his cue. Meanwhile, from all over Palestine and from Jewish communities scattered around the Mediterranean, individuals and groups made their way toward Jerusalem for another Passover. Whether Jesus would show himself, and if so what the authorities would do, were questions in all minds, as was the official order to report his hiding place (55–57).

Returning in good time to Bethany, Jesus was welcomed to an evening meal, perhaps the 'habdala', a Saturday supper 'separating' the sacred sabbath from the secular first day of the week. The unexpected reminder of the raising of Lazarus, so soon after the event, may have been inserted when sections of the Gospel were read in public worship (compare 11:2).

Martha was serving again (Luke 10:40), and Mary took opportunity to pay her never-to-be-forgotten tribute of love, understanding, and devotion. It was a costly tribute: 'nard' was an Indian plant, widely famous for its fragrant oil; 'pure' may indicate a plant species (in Greek), or be a rare word meaning 'genuine'. Three hundred pence was a year's wage for a farm labourer. It was a dangerous tribute, too, in view of the official order to report where Jesus was.

With the sisters' generosity, John deliberately contrasts the mean spirit of Judas. The accusation that he was a thief as well as treasurer must represent hindsight, based upon those thirty pieces of silver. This contrast, like the notice of Lazarus' presence at table, the fragrance filling the house, and Mary catching any falling drops for her own hair (she would not waste the costly oil, either) are details which almost guarantee personal reminiscence.

The moment was obviously of moving significance for Jesus. But it is not free of questions. The identification of this story with Luke 7:36–50, so making Mary of Bethany 'a woman of the city (streets)', and probably Mary Magdalene, is a persistent error, without foundation and full of problems. Luke's story and John's differ so widely that both cannot be true of the same incident. Christ's feet would be washed and anointed at every well-conducted house he visited. The heat, the state of the roads, and the use of light sandals, made the action the most natural and necessary welcome for any guest. Jesus expected it in a wealthy home (Luke 7:44–46), for its omission was ill-mannered; he did the service himself later (13:5; compare Psalm 23:5; Genesis 18:3–4; 19:2).

At Bethany, the exceptional feature was the costliness of the unguent used, and the profound insight expressed in Mary's care and devotion. She has read Christ's mind, felt his deep foreboding, understood the danger into which his return to Jerusalem has brought him. The other Gospels make clear that the male disciples have been quarrelling for weeks about which of them was to be greatest in Christ's kingdom: Mary feels the loneliness of his burdened spirit, and does 'a beautiful thing' (Mark 14:6).

John calls it a fragrant thing (3). The Jewish Talmud preserves the saying: 'A good unguent spreads from the bedroom to the dining hall, and so does a good name from one end of the world to the other' (compare Mark 14:9). A later writer says that Abraham lay like a jar of ointment in the corner of the room until God called him, then his fragrance became known. John was as aware of a homiletic allusion as anyone!

Judas' criticism should not surprise us. Those out of sympathy with Jesus can hardly approve 'extravagant' devotion to him. Worse even than a hireling, Judas cared neither for the shepherd, nor did he care for the poor; whatever motives prompted his betrayal of Jesus, to accept money for disloyalty does not suggest a caring, generous disposition. But Jesus' reply to Judas' criticism is less easy to understand. He defends the urgent, generous impulse that seizes the opportunity of showing loving sympathy (8), without thereby making extravagance an ideal of Christian life. It is easy to make 'constant demands' an excuse for never responding to immediate and fleeting opportunities for good. But 7 is very ambiguous.

Seven different translations of 7 may be defended. The main difficulty is that 'keep' may mean 'preserve, keep for an appropriate time' (the unguent); or 'observe, fulfil the duties of' (the sabbath, for example). Jesus reads into Mary's action a deep understanding of his mood and interprets the anointing as a preparation for burial. We are told that such jars of costly perfume were treasured against a coming marriage, or if that failed, for ultimate funeral purposes. Mary has foreseen Jesus' death, and knows that her brother's restored life has helped to bring it about.

It is tempting therefore to suppose that she should keep the ointment for the time when it will be needed. But this she has not done, and Jesus' words seem pointless—unless we assume some ointment remained unused. By John's account later, the anointing for actual burial was performed by Joseph of Arimathea and Nicodemus.

Since John, alone, places this anointing before Jesus' entry to Jerusalem, some have interpreted it as a preparatory 'coronation'. John might have thought that, but would Mary? Jesus did not (7).

Others choose the alternative translation, 'Let her alone, let her perform ('keep') the funeral custom (now, in preparation) for the day of my burial.' That is, Mary has read the future rightly, and has done what will need to be done while she still could. (The formal anointing of Jesus' body later would still be necessary, after death.) Such an act may sound strange, but it is close to Christ's words. Possibly such a meaning was not clearly in Mary's mind, until Jesus gave her act that interpretation.

Uncertainty of detail does not mar the beauty of Mary's tribute, or the significance of it for Jesus' sorrowing heart at that moment. The immediate outcome of the visit to Bethany is further opposition: the death warrant against Jesus was extended to include Lazarus, an act of blind, unjust, inexcusable violence. The authorities have by this time lost all credibility. Verse 11 implies (in Greek) a steady withdrawal of allegiance from the Jewish leaders and a steady increase of support for Jesus. This made possible the next, and final, step in Christ's challenge to the city.

The welcoming of pilgrims as they arrived for the great festivals, by the waving of palm branches (called 'hosannas') and shouts of 'save, we pray', was established custom from at least the time of Psalm 118, which describes in detail the ritual involved (Psalm 118:19–28). As NEB makes clear, in the psalm it is the blessing, not the coming, that is in the name of the Lord (compare 2 Samuel 6:18). The custom of greeting all the pilgrims thus implies this, though to Christian minds, there was indeed one among the crowd who came expressly 'in the Lord's name'.

For once again Jesus took advantage of a presented opportunity. A great crowd, already excited by rumours that Jesus would attend the feast, and by reports of the raising of Lazarus (9), found Jesus in their midst as they moved forward from Bethany towards Jerusalem (17–18). Others, hearing of his approach, went from Jerusalem to meet him

(13). So the customary cry of welcome became a special, popular acclamation celebrating the coming of the wonder-working prophet—that, at least.

It is scarcely possible to believe that Jesus did not foresee this. He certainly did nothing to avoid it. And while John says simply that Jesus 'found' a young ass, Mark and Matthew make quite clear that the 'finding' was elaborately pre-arranged, with password planned and permission promised. So Jesus rode into the city, and the crowd kept up its chanting (13), adding the words 'even the king of Israel'. Religious excitement deepened into patriotic fervour.

Such a move was extremely dangerous. In Galilee, after feeding the five thousand, Jesus had deftly handled the attempt to make him king on the people's own terms (6:15). Here, in the city, after the raising of Lazarus (John reiterates this point, 9, 17–18), it was much more perilous to claim kingship, much more difficult to insist upon his own terms.

The donkey, no military charger but a beast of burden and service, and the memory of Zechariah's prophecy, addressed to Jerusalem (15) enabled Jesus to say, unarguably, just what he wanted to say. He came peaceably, having salvation, lowly, and riding upon an ass. Any Jewish crowd would recognize the tableau, and know how the prophesy continues: 'I will cut off the chariot from Ephraim and the warhorse from Jerusalem; and the battle bow shall be cut off, and he shall command peace to the nations . . .' (Zechariah 9:9–10).

So at last the messianic claim was publicly and boldly made, and the messianic function defined as peace, lowliness, and service. And all done in a manner that no Jew could misunderstand, and no Roman could take exception to! The Pharisees certainly saw the point, and despaired (19). They knew themselves outwitted, and helpless.

Jesus had shown himself to be Messiah, yet no leader of fanatical Zealots, no militaristic son of empire-building David, nor yet a super-natural figure arriving on the clouds. He is the servant of the Lord, sent on mission, obedient, dependent, peaceable, speaking the words of God, doing the works of God in a needy world. The city had little choice left, and no excuse. The nation could accept him or reject him; but after this public demonstration they could not pretend to misunderstand him. And they dare not ignore him.

Suggestions for group discussion:

1 In John's representation Jesus was a formidable opponent, indomitable, daring, outwitting his adversaries, capitalizing his oppor-tunities, challenging hostility. Does this, in the mind of the group, ring true? Or have they a gentler conception of Christ?

2   What significance does the group see in the fact that, amid all the excitement and argument, quarrelling and danger of Jesus' last weeks, only one, and a woman, offered him the solace of sympathy and deep understanding? Are women (and poets?) better than most men as interpreters of Jesus?

The issue of the conflict   *John 12:20–50*

As though to underline the disparaging comment of the Pharisees (19), John records as the final incident of Jesus' public ministry the request of certain Greeks to see him. These were probably proselytes, in Jerusalem for Passover, who wished to understand the latest developments in their new religion. Curiously, we are not told if they met Jesus. John is concerned with their request, and its remarkable effect upon the master.

With their coming, the Jews' question 'Does he intend to go... among the Greeks and teach the Greeks?' (7:35) receives the answer 'No, they come to him!' And Jesus' words about 'other sheep not of this fold' and 'children of God scattered abroad' are now illumined and underlined. These Greeks were forerunners of many: the wider world was in truth knocking at Jesus' 'door' (10:9; note 'all men' 12:32).

The Greeks approached Philip, who sought Andrew's guidance, both men bearing Greek names and coming from the edge of Greek-speaking Decapolis (1:44). When these reported the request to Jesus his reaction was totally unexpected. The hour, long expected, had now come for him to be 'glorified' (for this 'hour' see 2:4; 7:6, 8, 30; 8:20; 12:23–27; 13:1; 17:1; compare 9:4–5; for the special meaning of 'glorified' see our introductory paragraphs, 'A tentative outline' about chapters 18–20).

Verses 24–26, though very condensed, are exceptionally important. At this crucial moment, at the end of his ministry, as death approached, Jesus reviewed the principles that had governed his life. Inevitably, these are the principles that must govern also lives that 'follow him'. Life must be devoted, surrendered, relinquished if need be, if it is to be fruitful (24). By death Jesus would be liberated from limitations of space and time to 'bear much fruit' in all the world and (through the Spirit, his 'other self') in all ages. That is how his dying-rising-ascending will attain glory.

Behind this surrender lay the deliberate choice of eternal values in preference to a life self-centred and world-conditioned (25; 15:19–20). In this choice the Greek ideal of moderation was not enough; one life or the other must be forgone utterly—'lost'. That is the essence of the Christian personal ethic. Moreover, any service of God's cause, or Christ's, rests upon personal loyalty, sustained by ever-closer identification with Christ (26; see 15:5; 17:24); the sole aim of all such service is the Father's approval (26).

Such were the principles by which Jesus lived, and for which he soon would die. Meanwhile his soul was troubled (27; 11:33, 38; 13:21). This is the nearest approach in this Gospel to the story of Gethsemane. In the traditions about Jesus as they reached John, place and details were fading, but the awful agony of spirit that Jesus underwent was clearly remembered, together with some of the words he used (27; 18:11). The struggle was intense, but the outcome never in doubt.

Jesus' 'No!' to the temptation to ask deliverance from that hour was as clear and decisive as 'not my will be done'. 'For this purpose I have come to this hour' recognizes as clearly that his whole mission implied this imminent suffering, death and glory. 'Father, glorify thy name' affirms yet again Christ's total obedience as the servant of the Lord (recall the commentary on 5:1–47).

God's response, 'I have glorified [my name]' signifies total approval of all Christ's words and works, performed 'to the Father's glory' (7:18; 11:4, 40; 17:4, and so on). And in the words 'I will glorify it again' lies the assurance that in spite of rejection, suffering and death, God will yet vindicate Jesus. Thus God set his seal, at this decisive moment, upon Jesus' past and future.

That moment was indeed laden with significance. It was so for Jesus, because his death would mean exaltation (32)—his cross would become a magnet drawing all men, though not all would yield and come. The moment was significant for the Jews, because at this point (according to John) Jesus closed his ministry to them, and hid himself from them (36). By John's time, the whole Church knew of Paul's doctrine that the turning from the Jews gave the Gentiles their opportunity (Acts 13:46; Romans 11:11, 17–25), but John does not suggest that; the Greeks have already come seeking Jesus.

The moment was significant, too, for the world and its supernatural 'ruler' (31; 14:30; 16:11). The divine vindication of Jesus implied of necessity the divine condemnation of all other forces that held the world in bondage.

Of course not all present understood the events in which they shared. It is useless to guess how the sound came (28), whether actual thunder (as Psalm 29:3–9), the reverberating echo of Jesus' 'glorify... glorify...' or 'the daughter of the divine voice' like the chirping of birds, of which the Rabbis spoke. But 29–30 plainly illustrate varying levels of spiritual perception reading different meanings into the same events. 'Thunder' is the sceptic's comment, explaining everything away. 'An angel' is the half-superstitious, half-religious interpretation, lacking conviction and commitment. 'This *voice...*' is the perception of the spirit always attuned to the Father's mind and heart.

John has already illustrated 'seeing and not perceiving' (9:39–41); now he illustrates the possibility of 'hearing and not listening'. Jesus' comment (30) probably renders a Hebrew expression meaning 'more for your sakes than for mine'; his faith needed no such reassurance (recall 11:42).

Jesus' reference to his death calls forth a scriptural 'poser' intended to divert attention from solemn themes. Whether conceived as son of David or as Son of man, the Messiah was expected to reign for ever (Isaiah 9:6–7; Ezekiel 37:25; Daniel 7:13–14), though various opinions were current as to how this could be. This puzzle is put to Jesus, but he refuses to be drawn into further argument. The time for that has passed, the nation's opportunity is slipping away, the light is fading (35–36), and soon darkness must fall upon those who prefer darkness—and who knows where they will end? But, for a while the choice remains, that those who will believe in the light may yet become 'sons of light' (compare Luke 16:8; 1 Thessalonians 5:5).

With that Jesus departs. He reappears in public only to be arrested (18:1–11).

Or does he? To whom is Jesus still speaking in 44–50? This is one instance where the suggestion that a paragraph has been misplaced in some early copy seems most plausible, though no existing copy offers evidence of it. The alternative explanation, that John saved Jesus' final words until after his own comments (37–43) seems less probable, and a very rude interruption!

Verse 44 follows smoothly upon the first sentence of 36, continuing the theme of 'light'. The warning that to reject Jesus is to reject God who sent him is pressed home for the last time. It is not with Jesus only that they must reckon, but with God: the light Jesus brings, the life he offers, what he says and how he says it (49 NIV, NEB), are all from God. This is Jesus' last word to Jewry: their decision will be judged by the truth and before God. It is noteworthy that in these final sayings, most of the themes of the book are plainly echoed and firmly summarized. With that urgent last appeal, it seems, 'Jesus ... departed, and hid himself from them.'

It is not surprising that at such a point John could not resist pausing to comment again on what he writes (37–43). He finds it incredible that such a ministry should end in quibbling, argument, and rejection. And he had lived (as we know) to see the unbelief of Jesus' contemporaries used as evidence that Jesus could not have been the Messiah. To this, he records the Christian answer: the Jews' own great prophet, Isaiah, had complained of their unbelief and blindness. It was nothing new for Jews to miss God's message; their own Scriptures foretold that they would. Indeed, they could not believe (39). As Jesus had told Nicodemus, Jewry could never, on its own level of insight and motive, attain Christ and the kingdom. It needed to be reborn from above.

Isaiah may have meant that nothing, not even the Jews' age-old intransigence, ever happens outside the will of God (40); for God made mankind free. It is certainly true that persistent refusal to believe can leave a soul incapable of believing. Jewish unbelief, therefore, proved nothing about Jesus' claims, but only about the stubbornness of human hearts. Isaiah's prophecies about this tended rather to confirm that Jesus was Messiah.

Of course John allows exceptions to the widespread unbelief (42). 'Many even of the authorities' would include Joseph of Arimathea, Nicodemus and those mentioned at 7:31; 8:30; 10:42; 11:45; 12:11. Fear kept many silent because of the threats of violence (42; 7:13; see on 9:22, 35). Such violent action only exposed the barrenness of all arguments against Jesus, but it intimidated those with much to lose. Behind all else lay the intense pride of Jewry (43). With this, whether expressed in nationalism, self-righteousness, or love of office, Jesus had repeatedly collided. John repeats the pun on 'Judah' (meaning both 'Jews' and 'praise'), which Jesus had alluded to (see 5:44).

John's reply to Jewish calumny would sound far more cogent to his contemporaries than it does to us, but his main contention is convincing enough: popular rejection proves nothing. That a person or a message finds little public favour has never been any criterion of truth, of importance, or of taste. Time tests truth, and by that test the claims of Jesus are abundantly verified.

But in his personal comment upon the close of Jesus' ministry John has linked Jesus directly with the great chapter in Isaiah which describes the suffering of the Servant of the Lord. This collocation of ideas almost certainly originated with Jesus, as a reinterpretation of messiahship, and it had become one of the central themes of apostolic Christianity (Acts 3:26; 4:30; 8:30–35; Philippians 2:5–11; 1 Peter 2:22–25, and at least thirteen echoes elsewhere in the New Testament).

John has insisted again and again that Jesus was the subservient, dependent, obedient servant of the Lord, sent on mission into the world (recall our introductory paragraphs, 'Remarkable disclaimers'). Within a very few verses, as the story moves towards the cross, John will vividly describe Jesus at work as servant of the Lord among the disciples. That cannot be accidental. It is the clue to John's account of the coming passion.

Suggestions for group discussion:

1   There is room for full and profitable discussion of 12:24–26 as expressing the essence of Christian life. What would the group add to complete the listed 'principles', or to elaborate each point?

2   Has John adequately explained the unbelief that rejected and crucified Jesus, in spite of the centuries of preparation for him? Would the modern world have understood Jesus better, sympathized more with his intentions, and accepted his claims?

4

Christ's Self-manifestation to His Own

John 13:1—17:26

John gives more than a fifth of his space to one evening's private conversation, in which Jesus reveals further his heart and purpose, his trust in his men, his expectation for the future. Among the most profound and precious in the New Testament, these five chapters are not, for all that, among the simplest to understand. But the reward gained by patience and reverence is very great.

The Greek Testament finds twenty paragraphs marking the separate steps in Jesus' discourse; RSV makes it twenty-three paragraphs, NEB discovers thirty-six steps, and NIV (if we ignore its preference for giving each speaker a separate paragraph), breaks the conversation into forty-three sections. In addition, there are two major, and very obvious 'jumps' in thought, that from 14:31 to 15:1, and that from 15:17 to 15:18. Plainly, the argument is not everywhere easy to follow, and it can be very misleading to imagine or invent connections where John has not made them clear. Yet it is difficult to accept that Jesus spoke incoherently. What has John done?

Careful readers soon notice that here Jesus touches upon some topic—the coming of the Spirit, prayer, peace, keeping his commandments, and the like—only to drop it, and take it up again later. The impression is thus created of 'rambling' talk, of thought moving in a circle. To collect what Jesus says on any one theme, we have to flit backwards and forwards between four overlapping chapters.

Very careful readers notice also a further curious fact: the first reference to such subjects falls in chapters 13—14; subsequent references to the same topics occur in chapters 15—16. This seems unimportant, until we realize that it occurs certainly fifteen times, probably seventeen times! In other words, while giving us some new sayings of Jesus, chapters 15—16 take us over much the same ground as chapters 13—14, elaborating the same topics.

Further, one does not even have to read carefully to notice that at 14:31 (the border-line between chapters 13—14 and chapters 15—16) no one takes any notice of Jesus' words. We might, in fact, pass straight from 14:31 to 18:1 with perfect smoothness. Instead, Jesus continues talking (and praying), at first on a new theme and then reverting to his earlier topics, for another three chapters.

Finally, while we are making these comparisons between what is said in the first pair of chapters and what is said in the second pair, we may notice one very strange thing: In 16:5 Jesus gently rebukes the Eleven in the words, 'None of you asks me, "Where are you going?" ', although at 13:36 Peter had asked precisely that, and at 14:5 Thomas had asked almost the same!

To remove these 'difficulties' some would straighten out this important discourse by radically re-arranging its paragraphs, bringing together all Jesus said on each separate topic, placing 16:5 before 13:36, placing 14:31 at the end, and so on. That involves much guesswork, and few would agree with any particular scheme. We remember that before reading became general memories were prodigious, and that Jesus promised the Spirit would bring all to the disciples' remembrance; yet we know that the Gospels were not dictated supernaturally, the evangelists recording the oral testimony of eyewitnesses as it circulated in the Church (Luke 1:1–4). The Spirit's encouragement and guidance was doubtless real, but not magical.

The simplest explanation of the puzzling features of John 13—16 is that John received more than one account of what was said in the Upper Room. Chapters 13—14 contains one account, brief and straightforward, showing the outline-pattern of Jesus' conversation, and ending with the suggestion that they all rise and go (14:31), which they did (18:1). But John had more information to share, filling gaps in the outline pattern, supplementing it on most of its topics. To preserve this information, John did not disturb the pattern of 13—14, but added footnotes to it, 'other things Jesus said in the course of the evening', so to speak. For one persuasive example, 15:1–11 seems obviously a footnote to 13:30–35.

No one would base upon this supposition any particular interpretation. Whatever value it has must appear as we study each section of the long conversation. The most one would claim is that it seems to offer one explanation of various odd details in these chapters—and if we reject it, we will find it difficult to discover a better one, or just be left with the problems. Even so, the 'difficulties' are small beside the enduring richness of this private table-talk of Jesus with his friends.

The manifold setting   *John 13:1–4*

The immediate setting for Jesus' frank self-disclosure is the night on which he was betrayed. The evening was filled with menace, the disciples' hearts with perplexity, foreboding, and fear. They ask: 'Lord, where are you going?' (13:36); 'Why cannot I follow you?' (13:37); 'What is this that he says to us, "A little while, and you will not see me?"' (16:17); 'We do not know what he means' (16:18).

The dawning realization that Jesus was about to leave them, that their hopes of power and pre-eminence in the coming kingdom might after all not be realized, that the danger they sensed overhanging Jesus might involve tragedy for themselves also—all found them wholly unprepared. 'I go away... You will see me no more...'—nineteen times in the course of that evening Jesus strove to prepare their minds, seven times he spoke of coming grief and tribulation, five times of betrayal and treachery. At one point, 'Judas went out, and it was night.'

Shut within that secret Upper Room Jesus talked of the outside 'world', naming it forty times and referring to it a further sixteen times. He spoke, not of God's love for it, or of the disciples' duty to serve it, but of the world's loving its own, coming under judgment, not knowing the Father or himself, never being able to bestow peace, or to receive the Spirit. He spoke especially of the world's hostility towards himself and his followers, and (four times) of its 'hatred'.

Such a world, with its evil 'ruler', awaits these men, planning rejection, persecution, for them as it plans death for him. In his closing prayer Jesus twice says, 'I am not praying for the world.' Thus, one overriding purpose of this evening's conversation was to stiffen the disciples' resolve, to offer comfort, the promise of over-coming, the assurance of inward peace, and (especially) to urge them to stand together. 'I tell you now, so that when it happens you may believe...' It is important to keep in mind, right through to chapter 17, this dark, menacing setting and mood of foreboding.

The wider setting is the long perspective of the future years, when these men must witness, labour, and suffer, amid changes they cannot foresee, in lands they have never visited, to peoples vastly different from themselves, and without his physical presence and leadership. If they fail, all that he has worked for and will suffer for will come to naught.

This forward vision is very clear in the words of Jesus' prayer, 'I do not pray for these only, but also for those who are to believe in me through their word...' But it also runs through these chapters. Jesus' concern is with the time between the advents, with the needs, dangers, and resources for the days between his 'going' and his coming again. Each of the other Gospels records, toward the end of Christ's ministry, his teaching about the future, and God's purpose for the world; John concentrates upon what Jesus has to say about the future of the Church.

We have to remember as we read that by the time John is writing decades of Christian experience, of the Church's world expansion, of life in the Holy Spirit, have given added significance and urgency to much that at the time the disciples heard with bewilderment and fear. We shall sometimes feel again that hindsight illumines memory, as we strive to catch the overtones and nuances of this, perhaps the most important conversation in history.

The immense significance of that evening's work is caught in the condensed phrases of 1–4. The English 'Now' here represents an almost negligible Greek word used simply to mark transition and contrast. Publicly, Jesus is rejected, and has retired; privately, something momentous was about to take place.

That momentous act of self-revelation is set against the background of the Passover, a time-note certainly, but never merely that. The city is crowded, excitement is running high, thoughts of ancient deliverance and present hope, of sacrifice and high devotion, stir many minds. And Jesus, the deliverer, and lamb of God, prepares quietly to fulfil yet another festival.

His self-revelation is set against the background of an 'hour' long awaited (1, see 12:23). All Jesus' life has been ordered by the Father, now the appointed pattern of his days nears its climax. His mission almost fulfilled, Jesus is about to return to the Father who sent him: it is not men's will that rules his life, but the Father's, and Jesus is ready.

His self-revelation is set, too, against the background of his undying love for these men (1). He loves his own as intensely as the world loves its own (15:19), but unchangeably, selflessly, to the end of time or to the uttermost degree (John's phrase is ambiguous). This personal tie, laden with the sadness of parting, added to the tension of the evening. There was however, an exception: the defection of Judas (2) added shock and shame to the disciples' grief. The loyalty implied in eating together did not bind them all. The devil prompts evil, but it requires a weak and willing heart to acquiesce before wrong is done, and in this instance it required also a stubborn resistance to the unfailing love which Jesus had shown to Judas as to the rest.

That background of cosmic, demonic evil (2) contrasts with Christ's self-disclosure. Around the supper table of a private home in Jerusalem, eternal issues were being fought out. Judas may be the agent, with a minor part to play; the real source of opposition to God's purposes is the age-long conflict of God with 'the adversary' ('the satan' in Hebrew), of light with darkness (1:5), of good with evil. Now on this last evening battle lines are drawn; the 'ruler' of the world plots against the Saviour of the world, and is about to be judged (12:31). He comes to grapple with Jesus, but finds no handhold in him (14:30).

We have not exhausted even yet these packed opening verses. Christ's self-manifestation is set, further, against the background of his Lordship over all: the Father had given all things into his hands (3). As he came to this hour and faced its dread outcome, Jesus was conscious of this, says John. Only such an inner awareness of the Father's favour could have sustained Jesus in that troubled but indomitable calm which carried him through that night and day. Both Matthew and Paul emphasize this exalted gift by which the Father rewarded the obedience of his servant (Matthew 28:18; Philippians 2:9–11; compare Hebrews 1:3; 12:2).

Finally, and wonderfully, this evening's self-disclosure was set against the background of the whole redemptive movement that brought Christ from the glory he had with God before the world was made (3; 17:5), to earth with its insults, humiliation, rejection and death—and which would take him back again to glory and the Father. As they gathered for the last time together before the cross, the saving purpose of God moved a giant stride forward. Something truly momentous was afoot, the saving of the world.

With so magnificent a preamble, what John had to tell had to be magnificent too. And it is. But it began so strangely: Jesus 'rose from supper, laid aside his garments, and girded himself with a towel... poured water into a basin, and began to wash the disciples' feet'!

Suggestions for group discussion:

1 John 13—17 are, to many Christians, favourite chapters for quiet devotional meditation, 'retreats', uplifting sermons and comforting promise-cards. The atmosphere of fear, foreboding, challenge and change which we have described is very different. Which is the right approach?
2 Does the group find 13:1–4 impressive, arresting attention, kindling expectation of something supremely important, or merely mystifying?

The feet-washing and after   *John 13:3–35*

Supper being ready, Jesus waited for the customary courtesy (see commentary on 12:3) that should precede every such meal (on the nature of this one, see our introductory paragraphs, 'A different story?' at end). Those whose ritual purification had been performed in outlying 'immersion pools' would still need to wash their feet after walking into the city (10). In such company, lacking servants, the service normally fell to the youngest present. No one offered.

Luke reveals that the disciples were disputing which should be greatest (Luke 22:24–28), and Jesus had said 'Let the greatest among you become as the youngest, and the leader as one who serves ... I am among you as one who serves.' John omits the saying, but describes the dramatic deed that says it all. But not one in that circle was in the mood to kneel before the rest. Jesus does so, girded like a slave, and does not omit Peter (who would deny him), or Thomas (who would doubt), or Judas (who would betray him). All had watched a woman do this for Jesus: they refused, even for him.

The silent rebuke partly explains Peter's shamed protest (6, 8). So does the implication that Peter needed such service. Most Christians, even yet, are more ready to do things for Christ than to acknowledge their need of what only he can do for them! It requires genuine humility to let Christ serve us. Peter had that still to learn.

Jesus insists, finishes the task, resumes his robe and his place at table. No one, apparently, dared offer now to wash his feet. Into the embarrassed silence Jesus dropped his searching question (12). They had watched, but had they seen the point? Prestige does not preclude service (13–14): he had provided example and motive—the true Christian motive of gratitude. The were called not simply to admire and imitate, with self-conscious virtue, but to remember how they had been served, and to serve with thankfulness (15).

The moral lesson was timely (compare Matthew 11:29, and the echo of the story in 1 Peter 5:5). But a moral lesson hardly needed that magnificent preamble. Nor does it explain the strange remark in verse 7. Still less did it call for the warning of 8. These pregnant words leave no doubt that some washing other than clean feet, other than ritual purification for the festival, was in Jesus' mind, as Peter realized (9).

We are reminded at once that the story of the feet-washing is set between Isaiah's words about the servant of the Lord (John 12:38) and Jesus' words about servants and those sent (16). We are watching the sent servant fulfilling his mission of service: 3–5 is the very portrait of the servant-Messiah.

And the form of his service of humankind is equally significant. Jesus is seen here not healing, preaching, praying, but cleansing soiled humanity. This is the 'washing' without which we can have no part in him, the 'washing' which the disciples could not then understand but would understand afterward, the 'washing' which must not be refused, and glimpsing which, Peter longed should be total.

The word 'wash' occurs eight times in 5–14. In the subsequent verses, Jesus cleanses the apostolic band of its one unworthy member (11, 27), in 15:2 he speaks again of the need to 'cleanse' (Greek) the vine of God. Later Jesus prays that the disciples may be kept from evil, and sanctified as he had sanctified himself. And all this is said under the shadow of Passover and the need of purification for the festival (11:55; 18:28). On that day he would die as the lamb of God which bears away the sin of the world. Such is the servant's task in a sinful world.

Admittedly, this whole notion sounds strange to us. And unwelcome. This is because the thought of the holiness of God has largely faded from modern Christianity. To Jesus' generation, and to John's readers, the need of cleansing was constantly brought to mind by required rituals of hand-washing, bathing, washing of clothes and the like before any religious observance (see Mark 7:3–4; Hebrews 10:22). Prophets, too, had emphasized the need of cleansing (Ezekiel 36:25; Zechariah 13:1; Isaiah 1:16–18). The practice of proselyte baptism, like the Baptist's rite, underlined it further. To Jewish minds, a religious leader with basin and towel demanding purification was no enigma. But as applied to Messiah, the image was startling, incredible.

And to our minds—what does such cleansing mean? Later, Jesus will say that the disciples are made clean by the word he has spoken to them, and will pray that they might remain sanctified in the truth which is God's word. That cleansing of mind, imagination, and understanding is at any rate not difficult for us to comprehend, nor will anyone daily fretted by the prevailing climate of falsehood and filth question the need for it. But more was implied.

Peter's outburst (9) recalls the Rabbi's demand, when proselytes were baptized, for total cleansing (complete immersion, nude, with unbound hair and unclenched hands). Jesus's reference to 'bathing' (10) likewise evokes the thought of baptism, called 'washing' in Acts 22:16; 1 Corinthians 6:11; Titus 3:5; Ephesians 5:26; recall John 3:5, 22; 4:1). By John's time, Christian baptism was the appointed entrance into Church membership, signifying cleansing from past defilements by repentance, faith, dying and rising with Christ, and enduement with the Spirit. No Christian at the end of that first century would read John's words in this passage without remembering his own cleansing in the sacrament of baptism.

But it would probably not be his immediate thought. In that apostolic Church the death of Christ for the world's redemption was still interpreted in sacrificial language, as 'expiation', the cleansing of defilement and removal of 'uncleanness' in God's sight by means of appropriate offerings. In the world of Jesus and of John, literal sacrifices were inseparable from religion, whether Jewish (Hebrews 9:18-22) or pagan (Acts 14:11–13; 1 Corinthians 10:20 and so on), and sacrificial conceptions persisted in the Church long after animal sacrifice was left behind. We meet them in the eucharist, for example (Matthew 26:28; 1 Corinthians 11:25) and in explanations of the gospel like Romans 3:25; Ephesians 1:7; 1 Peter 1:18–19; Hebrews 9:11–14, 23–28; Revelation 12:11.

Paul speaks expressly of Christ our paschal lamb sacrificed for us, in connection with our cleansing (1 Corinthians 5:6–8), which is very close to John's thought. Closer still are the explicit statements, in the 'note' associated with John's Gospel, 'the blood of Jesus his Son cleanses us from all sin', 'he is the expiation for our sins . . . also for the sins of the whole world', 'God . . . loved us and sent his Son to be the expiation for our sins' (1 John 1:7; 2:2; 4:10). There is no doubt that this is how cleansing was thought of in the Johannine school.

John introduces his narrative of the passion of Christ with the kneeling figure of the servant who cleanses. The time according to John is Passover eve, and on the following day the Lamb of God will bear away the sin of the world in his death. Remembering this, can we doubt that this cleansing, too, of the defiled conscience by expiation is also in John's mind as he writes verses 3–11? It may well have been suggested to John by his recent allusion to Isaiah's song of the servant, with its nine sacrificial phrases describing the servant's suffering (12:38).

Such terms are now 'dead metaphors' to those who never saw an animal sacrificed, but the truth they once conveyed is inescapable. In God's world evil cannot be ignored, excused, condoned as though it does not matter, and divine forgiveness is no make-believe disguising or denying unpleasant facts about human behaviour. To be worthy of God, even mercy must recognize, admit and condemn evil, and forgiveness rest upon expiation accomplished, atonement made, judgment acknowledged. By his confronting sin, bearing it and dying for it, Jesus 'washed clean' all who repent and believe: that is the deepest meaning of his washing the disciples' feet.

More immediately, at that supper table, another kind of cleansing was also necessary. That all-important group, the nucleus of the Church that was to be, contained one whose heart was not yielded to Christ, who indeed 'had no part' in Jesus (8). The disciple band, too, must be 'cleansed' (so 10–11).

When a woman anointed Jesus' feet and he spoke of his death, Judas went 'then' (Mark 14:10) to plot against Jesus with the priests. The sight of Jesus kneeling before them all with basin and towel, and his talk of being a servant (15–16) was the last straw, and led directly to the actual betrayal. This was not at all the kind of Messiah Judas expected, wanted, or would follow.

Jesus had to deal with Judas, but also with the Eleven, preparing them for the shock of this defection. The hint in 10 (which John explains for us!), the reminder in 17 ('if you do . . .'), prepare for the still vague warning in 18, before the bald announcement in 21. The shock will be slightly lessened if the Eleven remember afterwards that Scripture foretold such an event (18; by Middle Eastern custom, eating bread together pledged loyalty; the lifting of the heel pictures a normally quiet ox or mule unexpectedly lashing out at its driver; Psalm 41:9).

Besides, they must remember afterwards that Jesus knew what was going on. By speaking of it beforehand, he robbed the betrayal of any later reflection on himself as one greatly deceived (19). He chose them all (18; 6:70), and did so knowing what was in men (2:25). In choosing Judas he made no mistake, and certainly did not entrap him into a false position. Judas had qualities that might make a disciple, and was given the same opportunities and privileges as the rest. His final remorse reveals what he might have become.

But he went wrong. Though Judas became the agent of forces stronger than himself (2, 27; Mark 14:10–11), it was with his consent; he plotted, he accepted payment, he betrayed. The event was a warning to them all (20, Greek), that to receive or reject Jesus was to receive or reject God. (The beginning of verse 20 seems irrelevant here, and may have crept in from a copyist's memory of Matthew 10:40–41.)

Jesus dealt equally carefully with Judas, being deeply troubled for him (21). By this moment Judas must have realized that Jesus knew all. He at any rate recognized the warnings. The disciples did not immediately suspect Judas (22), and Jesus was careful not to arouse their hostility towards him. Nor will he force Judas into an irrevocable decision. The whispered comments and silent beckoning were further warning, shared only with the trusted. The giving of the first, choice morsel to Judas, as to a guest, was a last veiled appeal (23–26; on 'the beloved disciple' see our introductory paragraphs, 'Why doubt the tradition?').

The result was a change of expression, a flashing glance perhaps, that betrayed obdurate rejection, and Jesus met it with veiled but equally firm expulsion (27). The Eleven were ready with plausible explanations of Judas' leaving (almsgiving was a required element of Passover ritual). Had they guessed the truth, Judas might not have got away unharmed. Like all self-exclusion from grace, the night into which Judas stepped was also divine judgment (28–30).

As the door closed behind Judas so it closed upon Jesus' earthly life. This was the awaited hour. Jesus immediately accepts and announces the situation, setting it firmly in the context of the glory now awaiting him. But it means departure and separation. The declaration is made plainly, even baldly, and the time left for final instructions is very short, only long enough for Judas to report Jesus' presence in the city and summon the guard. Jesus had much to say, and they must listen (31–33).

First, they simply must learn the lesson of Judas' desertion. There must be no more defections. The future depends utterly upon the loyalty of the Eleven to each other and to him. He therefore commands it (34). Quarrelling about precedence, fear of the outside world, the threat of persecution, any cooling of love for him, all will drive them apart. And they must not part one from the other.

This is not the 'greatest' commandment, old as Leviticus and renewed in the divine kingdom, requiring love of one's neighbour. This is the special, urgent new commandment, limited to brethren, an internal loyalty demanded by a new and perilous situation and an evil example. From that night onwards, the Eleven must be bound in love together as never before.

This love of the brethren is no more sentiment of Christian friendliness, 'openness', 'togetherness', but an attitude, a resolve, far more radical, enduring, costly in days of persecution, yet indestructible. It constitutes that solidarity of Christians against a hostile world which later astonished the pagans, as Jesus said it would (35).

The measure, and the quality, of that mutual love was to be as his own love for them (34), honest, unshakeable, faithful in dealing with weaknesses and faults, yet enduring 'to the uttermost and to the end'. This Christian love is therefore not blind, romantic, sentimental; it has little if anything to do with liking one another. It is a mutual acceptance and valuation of each other as brothers and sisters, for whom Christ died. By such unbreakable loyalty of Christians to each other the world will recognize the unique influence of Jesus upon them (35).

Secondly, unless (unlike Judas) they all abide in him as branches in . . . But Jesus was interrupted.

Suggestions for group discussion:

1   The disappointment of Judas in a Messiah who could talk of dying, and wash people's feet, raises the question of what sort of Christ we want—a political liberator? a world-ruler? a Christ whose judgment will slay the wicked? a gentle pacifist? an other-worldly philosopher? a triumphalist advent king? or what?
2   Has Jesus' expulsion of Judas anything to teach us about Church discipline? Has the new commandment anything to teach us about denominationalism?

Four interruptions   *John 13:36—14:31*

Before Jesus could proceed with the second lesson to be drawn from Judas' defection, *Peter interrupted*, belatedly catching up with the topic-before-last, to ask where Jesus was going. As at 1:38, Jesus replied to the intention behind the question, which becomes clear in 37 with the rash undertaking to die with Jesus rather than fail (as Judas had done?). This self-confidence could not be allowed to pass.

Passionate, impulsive, well-meaning, but readier to promise than to perform, Peter was not yet 'rock', and must be brought to self-understanding. Hence the warning (38), which appears to shock Peter into silence until 18:15. Yet the fact that Jesus had known beforehand that he would disown Jesus, and had not disowned or excluded him, must afterwards have brought some comfort to the broken-hearted apostle.

Then Peter (and the rest, Greek) are given the answer to Peter's question. The disciples must not let themselves be troubled (contrast 13:21), because Jesus is going to 'the Father's house', to prepare for them and then return to receive them into a fellowship that will not again be broken. 'My Father's house' in 2:16 meant the temple, where God dwells. 'Rooms' means 'places to dwell' (so NEB; in 23 RSV has 'home' for the same Greek word; the familiar 'mansions' is a Latin distortion). Jesus is returning home, where there is ample room for all, and will make ready for them lodging, meals, and welcome (the meaning of 'prepare a place', see Psalm 23:5–6, and note 'standing' to welcome in Acts 7:55).

Varied translations and text of 14:1–2 all imply that the disciples' assurance of this must rest firmly upon Jesus' integrity; they must simply believe him. RSV makes 2 a question, presumably referring back to 13:36. NIV prefers 'I would have told you. I go . . .'; NEB has 'I should have told you; for I am going . . .' Similar difficulties confuse verse 4, though again the meaning is clear. The disciples should know by now that his way to the Father will be by death and resurrection.

All this, the eternal home, ample room, welcome, fellowship, a rendezvous with Christ that shall not end, constituted the argument for believing in him and not letting their hearts be troubled. Neither the menacing world outside, nor their inner fears, nor Caesar, Caiaphas, Pilate, Judas, the prince of this world, together, will prevent their meeting again, beyond the imminent separation, and beyond reach of evil, harm, and death.

This was where he was going, and they know the way . . .

But *Thomas interrupted*, not having followed Jesus' meaning very closely. That one passed through death to Sheol was obvious, but—to God? Again Jesus answers the thought behind the question. He speaks of that crucial but daunting central issue of life, the search for God. How shall a man come, here or hereafter, not only to the Father's house but to the Father? To that question there could be but one reply: the way to God is by Christ; no one comes by any other way (5–6).

RSV, NEB, NIV add, with the Greek, 'and the truth and the life'. Did Jesus add that 'for completeness', though Thomas had not enquired for more? Or do truth and life describe the way, as they might well do in the Aramaic which Jesus spoke (compare 'the way of truth', 'the living way')? Possibly so: 'I am the true and living way' would neatly contrast Christ, the living avenue to God, with the false way of paganism and the dead way of current Judaism.

The difference in meaning is small: 7 emphasizes that to know Christ is to know the Father, and to know Christ must mean to know the truth of his words, the quality of his life. So to let his way guide our feet, his truth fill our minds, his life continually renew our spirit, is to know God, and eternal life. That is Jesus' meaning, however he originally expressed it. Had the Eleven understood Jesus as they should have done, they would have known God in him (7; so 8:19).

From this evening, knowing Jesus better, they would so know God...

But here *Philip interrupted.* Jesus was thinking too fast for him. Taking up Jesus' last words he voiced the deepest longing of the religious soul in all generations, from Moses (Exodus 33:18) to the mystics, the longing for an individual, unmediated, experience of God. John has insisted that no one has attained that vision (1:18; 5:37; 6:46); pagan 'mystery religions' offered it as the climax to elaborate initiation. Faced with the fears and uncertainties of that fateful night, Philip desires not miracle or spectacle but certainty and moral assurance. 'Show us the Father, and we shall be all right!' John's readers, too, still enduring a hostile, changing world, would understand the longing.

Jesus' immediate reply is a sad echo of 7: 'to fail to see God in Jesus is to fail to know Jesus'. Verses 9–11 encapsulate the whole message of John: listen, watch, believe, and you will see God.

Jesus turns to the Eleven ('Believe you me...' in Greek is plural), and to the future when his words, deeds and presence will no longer be with them to be observed. Jesus analyses the continuing spiritual experience in which God will still be known.

▷ *Its basis is belief, at first perhaps in what his works reveal (11). That is not the highest faith, but it can lead to deeper understanding. The term here is 'works', not signs, as if to stress the divine, positive quality of all Jesus has done (so 5:36; 10:37–38). Faith is insight, a kind of seeing; a desiring, patient, accepting faith will see God.*

▷ *The outworking of that continuing experience will be in Christlike deeds, 'doing what is true', 'deeds wrought in God' (12; see 3:20–21). God is known as often in involvement with others' needs, in noble activity, as he is known in intellectual contemplation or emotional excitement. 'To those who obey him he will reveal himself in the toils, the conflicts, the sufferings which they shall pass through in his fellowship . . . and they shall learn in their own experience who he is' (Schweitzer). Learning so of Jesus, they learn of God.*

▷ *The inner side of that continuing experience is prayer of a new richness and power (13). Requested of the Father in Christ's name, it is granted by the Father through the action of Christ ('I will do it.') In such gracious accessibility and generosity, God will be glorified. Of course, not every trivial, thoughtless, selfish plea will be successful, but whatever request is worthy of having Christ's name appended to it. To ask what he will approve, is to ask what he is already eager to give, as soon as we are ready to receive. They who so pray will surely know God.*

In such belief, action and prayer, God will still be known though Christ is gone from sight. The record of Jesus' words and deeds will remain: but their meaning must 'come alive' in personal experience. If, with Philip, we still ask 'Show us the Father . . .', the short answer must be, 'Look at Christ, believe, work and pray as he approves, and God will make himself known.'

At this point, Jesus appears to resume what he was going to say when Peter interrupted him (13:36). Verse 15 could be the end of the reply to Philip, but it comes suddenly, without mention of the Father, and reintroduces momentarily the idea of commandments, which had been Jesus' subject at 13:35. We might paraphrase it: 'As I was saying, love for me will make loyalty among you all an obligation; I command it.' When mutual attractiveness, or plain expediency, fail to hold them together, obedience must.

Such 'commanding' is mentioned in John's Gospel twelve times (and fourteen times in the brief 1 John). It provides the ethical rigour which Johannine Christianity would otherwise lack. 'Love for Jesus' easily descends to sentimentality; obedience without love is not Christian, but 'love' without obedience is self-delusion (note 21).

Jesus' next theme in preparation for the future is the replacement of himself on his going by 'another' counsellor, the Spirit of truth. He too is the gift of the Father, as was Jesus (3:16). He will not depart, but remain for ever. In some sense, the Spirit is Jesus' 'other self', since Jesus can say 'he dwells with you, and will be in you' (16–17), and add, 'I will not leave you desolate; I will come to you' (18).

The Spirit, then, will be to the disciples all that Jesus has been, teaching, guiding, encouraging in all new situations. As the world has never seen, known, or welcomed Jesus, so it cannot receive his Spirit. In this way they will not be left friendless or leaderless; instead, his 'going' will prove to be a 'coming', into clearer knowledge, closer fellowship, and deeper love.

John adds considerably to the New Testament's teaching about the Spirit (1:32–33; 3:5; 7:39; 14:26; 15:26; 16:7–15; 20:22). Three times he is called 'Holy Spirit'; more often 'Spirit of truth', stressing his intellectual ministry (teaching, reminding, guiding into truth). Still more often John speaks of the 'Paraclete', variously translated as 'Comforter', one called alongside to fortify, encourage; or Counsellor, advocate, one called alongside to defend, to speak up for one in trouble, a friend of the accused, a friendly witness—contrast 'the Satan', adversary, accuser (Revelation 12:10). In 16:7–11 the Spirit becomes Prosecutor, one speaking for God.

By such continuing spiritual experience, and by the inward ministry of the Spirit, believers will assuredly know the Father. The world will see Jesus no more, but disciples will 'see' him more clearly than ever, and live because he lives (18). As to fellowship with Jesus, they will in future understand more perfectly the intimate unity of the Father, the Son, and themselves (20). As to love, those who know and observe his commands, so proving their love for him, will experience the love of the Father and of Christ in a clearer-than-ever understanding (21).

Here the longing of Philip receives its fullest reply. God is spirit: any request like 'Show us the Father' can be answered only in terms of fellowship, knowledge, indwelling, as the Father (23), the Son (18), the Spirit (16) come to make themselves known in ongoing Christian experience. A prophet had promised that all shall know God, from the least of them to the greatest of them (Jeremiah 31:34); as men and women live by belief, work, and prayer, so God comes as Father, Son, Spirit, and the prophecy is abundantly fulfilled.

Suddenly, *Judas interrupts*—the other Judas. We know nothing else about him, not even if he is the son (or brother) of James (Luke 6:16), or the Thaddeus (or Lebbaeus) of Matthew 10:3. Only that he was a disciple, and he interrupted Jesus.

He too seized upon something Jesus had just said, possibly thinking it indicated a change from public to private ministry (22). Judas' question, like Philip's, voiced a widespread feeling, which agitated the Church in John's day and has done so ever since. How is it that some can claim a spiritual certainty which others never attain? How do some reach living faith about Jesus' claims and his saving power, while so many can make nothing of them?

The answer lies (again, see commentary on 3:19–21) in moral predisposition and insight. Those who admire what Christ stood for, and desire it ardently, who treasure his vision and his teaching (23), will move forward to experience God's love, and know the divine indwelling which makes all clear and certain. Those whose life-set is against all Jesus stood for, miss that experience. For all Christ taught and demonstrated was from God (24).

It must be repeated that this predisposition is not a question of deserving. Spiritual enlightenment may come to the prodigal in the farthest country, aware of his misery, or to the proud Pharisee, 'chief of sinners', kicking against the goad. Nor, certainly, is it a question of intellect; in this realm the simplest often see farthest. Singleness of heart, sincerity in seeking, and a teachable spirit, are the obvious predisposing qualities that prepare for the divine approach (23). God loves the world, but only those willing to be loved will know it; God would come to all, but only those who welcome him make him at home in their lives.

Verses 25 and 30 seem plainly to indicate a closing summary, and the content of 26–30 tends to confirm that. The last words of 31 show that Jesus has completed his instructions, and is ready to move.

To the promise of the Spirit in 16–17 Jesus now adds that the Spirit's ministry will help to conserve all that the disciples have experienced with Christ, bringing them a teaching-remembrance, an interpretative recall, of all they have heard and seen. So any fear that, in losing Christ's presence, they will lose all that they have so slowly gained, is fully provided against.

The bequest of peace recalls 14:1, and adds, in view of the disciples' remaining fears, that the peace Jesus gives is of a quality which the world, or circumstances, could never bestow (27). It is a peace inwardly conditioned, a poise that never panics, a resilience that never loses its resolve. No stoic pride could match the invincible faith of the early Christians, nor could the watching world understand it. In a sufficient phrase Jesus called it 'my peace'. So fortified, they need never 'play the coward' (27, literally).

'You heard me say to you, I go away ...' recalls 13:33 and 14:3, this time to set Jesus' departure in a different light. The disciples' reaction had been dismay; if they had had as much thought for him as for themselves, they would have rejoiced for him, that he was returning to the Father, the greatest of all. His departure was no defeat, no retreat, no tragedy, but the culmination of his mission.

They would remember later that he had foreseen all, and that in spite of all appearances he himself remained in command. No agency in this world, not even the reputed ruler of this world, could snatch the initiative from Christ's hands; he dies in obedience to the Father's will (30–31; 10:18). Even the world that now rejects him will then realize how he loved the Father.

A moving close to one account of the final self-disclosure of Jesus to his own.

'Rise, let us go hence' (31) was doubtless a common enough phrase at the break-up of any domestic gathering. Here, it gains weight from remembering what they were going forth to, as 18:1 indicates. It is curious that in Matthew and Mark the same words close Christ's conversation in Gethsemane. One wonders if the simple phrase was imprinted on the mind of the Church as expressing the calm resolve with which Jesus faced his death. It would provide an inspiring example to every persecuted Christian as his own end drew near.

Suggestions for group discussion:

1   Jesus' provision for the demanding days to come was mainly the loyalty of disciples to one another against the world, and the promise of the Spirit's leadership and power. In the group's opinion, which do we most lack?

2   The peace which Jesus promised for the turbulent days ahead was a paradoxical serenity amid storm. Does the group think that the modern Christian's emphasis upon keeping the peace with all men, whatever the compromise involved, was what Jesus meant? Does Jesus, in these chapters, provide sufficient grounds for such peace?

Three footnotes   *John 15:1—16:4*

First footnote

The Greek word for 'prunes' (2) is from the same root as 'clean' in 13:10–11; the statement in 3 plainly echoes that in 13:10; the removal from the vine of the fruitless branch is clearly one way of describing the expulsion of Judas from the apostolic circle. For these reasons it seems obvious that Jesus had intended to say that the second lesson to be drawn from Judas' defection was the necessity of abiding in him, as a fruitful branch within God's vine. But Peter had interrupted. Now Jesus resumes his theme. He had publicly applied to contemporary Jewry Isaiah's parable of the vineyard in which, despite all his care, God had been deeply disappointed (Isaiah 5; Mark 12:1–12). Here, privately, Jesus applies the same imagery to himself and his disciples, the new 'true' vine of God, replacing the profitless vine of Israel. It was an old and prized metaphor (Jeremiah 2:21; Hosea 10:1; Psalm 80:8–13): vine leaves appeared on Maccabean coins; a golden vine adorned the temple gate. Jesus is making a large and provocative claim.

But the fruitfulness of this new vine, too, would depend upon the branches clinging to the main trunk, and one has already broken away, withered, been 'gathered . . . and burned'. Four operations are named (6); 'cast forth' implies not outgrowth but the slow, secret severance from the trunk that is only made evident later by its fruitlessness, then by withering. In Judas' case, the severance lay in loss of sympathy with Jesus, as at Bethany.

This is the human explanation of a disciple's defection. Judas first inwardly withdrew loyalty and trust from Jesus; then openly criticized the devotion Mary showed to him; then plotted, decided and acted against Jesus, as he thought on his own initiative. The divine explanation goes further: God is the vinedresser (1), and the pruning knife is in his hand. Knowing the breach, and the fruitlessness, God has through the action of Jesus cleaned away the withering branch.

Even onlookers see the effects of withering faith. 'They gather' (6, Greek) the useless branches and burn them, for vine wood has no other use (see Ezekiel 15:1–8). As Jesus spoke, the vacant place at the table made silent comment on his words. But, onlookers apart, the vineyard is God's, and the future of Christ's cause depends upon the branches abiding in the vine. This is repeated emphatically (4–5). There must be no more defections because God expects fruit, much fruit (5), more fruit (2), lasting fruit (16).

What that fruit is to be is not clearly described. Verse 5 suggests it will include things done; 7 appears to add a fruitful prayer-life, as Christ's teaching informs and enriches prayer; 8 adds such quality of living as befits disciples and glorifies God. Verse 11 implies that, as in any Middle Eastern vineyard, the fruit harvest is the occasion of abounding joy. Perhaps the form which Christian fruitfulness takes must vary with the background, the circumstances, the talents and inclination of every Christian. But one way or another, abiding in Christ will ensure enhanced and useful living.

What then is 'abiding'? Verse 5 stresses the mutual indwelling of Jesus and his men; 7 mentions the teaching of Jesus dwelling in the disciples' minds, and abiding by active prayer; 9–10 extends abiding to include keeping ourselves, by careful obedience, within the circle of Christ's love and God's (compare Jude 21). Verse 10 stresses commandments, because in this close union Jesus remains master.

Perhaps again the form of our abiding in Christ cannot be defined precisely for every Christian. Some will find one method of worship and devotion helpful, some another. Behind the figure Jesus is using lies the great truth that fills John's Gospel. In 6:57, life flows from the Father through the Son into all who will receive it. In 15:9, love flows out of the Father through Christ into the experience of the disciples. In the figure of the vine, fruit-bearing energy issues from God through the ministry of Jesus to nourish every branch-disciple who abides in him. How that life, love, energy will express itself in varied individuals will depend on many personal factors—capacity, education, tastes, temperament, conscience—but it is there to be appropriated by any who seek to bear fruit for God. Judas failed so to abide, and proved fruitless; the lesson must not be lost upon the rest. Nor upon their successors.

Second footnote

The theme suddenly changes. Three references to 'commanding' and two to loving one another, show that 12–17 is a footnote to 13:34–35—something further Jesus said, when he was speaking earlier about his new commandment. It was not Judas' defection alone, but the dangers ahead for them all, which made mutual loyalty essential. Their love would be tested when they stood together before persecutors, or sheltered those fleeing from persecution, so risking their own lives (see Hebrews 13:1–3; also 1 John 3:16, a clear echo of John 15:13).

Though Jesus' own death is not mentioned explicitly, it is obviously in mind as he goes on to describe the love he has for these his friends ('as I have loved you' of 13:34). This friendship which binds them all together does not preclude Jesus' commanding obedience; on the other hand, he asks no blind servitude, as of slaves, but a mutual confidence and a shared understanding of God's will, as between friends.

And it rests upon his deliberate choice and commissioning of them to bear fruit for God, that is, on something deeper and stronger than their own choice. This guarantees his own loyalty to them, and his readiness at all times to support their appeals to God for help in the work appointed them.

Friendship was highly valued in Graeco-Roman society, and its obligations were accorded high priority, perhaps because companionship was usually sought outside the home; Christian marriage of equal partners was a new idea. Some of John's Gentile readers would therefore appreciate the language of 12–17. But it is almost unique in the New Testament, where all other instances of the word are secular and social, except James 2:23 and 4:4, which contrast friendship with God and with the world. In Jesus' words friendship is triangular: 'any friend of Jesus is a friend of mine'.

In spite of 13, Christians did call themselves 'slaves of Christ' (Romans 1:1 and frequently; see 1 Corinthians 7:22). Perhaps until John wrote they did not know this saying of Jesus. By John's time the large number of (literal) slaves within the Church had become a ground of criticism in Graeco-Roman society. John may have had this in mind when recording how Jesus insisted the 'slave' was not an appropriate term for those who enjoy his friendship. He valued them far more highly than that.

Third footnote

Again the theme changes suddenly: 15:18—16:4 plainly develops Jesus' thought about the world in 14:17, 19, 22–24, 27, and 15:20 actually quotes 13:16. These are further reflections on a topic already touched upon, the hostility of that menacing world which has already swallowed Judas, will frighten Peter into denial, and which neither knows nor can receive the Spirit of truth.

The picture is of two mutually exclusive communities together within the same society: one chosen out of the world (19), serving Christ's aims (20), not of the world's kind (19), having been with Christ from the beginning (27); the other rejecting and persecuting Christ (20), not knowing God (21; 16:3), having now no excuse for its sinfulness (22, 23).

It is 'as truly the nature of the world to hate as of Christians to love', as John might say; and disciples must not be surprised that they inherit, when Christ has departed, all the hatred that the world heaped upon him. This will arise, partly because they are 'different', partly through envy of the Christian's privileges, but mostly because they are identified with Jesus (39; compare Colossians 1:24; 1 Peter 4:12–13).

The persisting enmity towards Jesus, and towards all who are his, is largely due to ignorance of God (21; 16:3), but also because his life and teaching have exposed the world's sinfulness, its predisposition towards evil (22, 24; 3:19–20). Yet, in the last analysis, this was no reason for hating him who was sent to reveal God and to remove sin (25). The quotation (Psalm 69:4; 35:19) reveals that the Jewish world is mainly before Christ's mind.

For all that, God still loves the world (3:16); Jesus was sent into the world, and disciples must witness to it; it must not be despised or abandoned. God gives the promised Counsellor to witness, along with the disciples, to the world (26–27). There is still hope, then, for some who are as yet 'in the world'.

But meanwhile Jesus warns them, with utter realism, of trouble ahead, not to discourage but to forearm (16:1); 'falling away', 'go astray' (NIV), 'breakdown of faith' (NEB), all treat the Greek word as a metaphor, but the literal meaning (from the trigger-stick of a snare), namely 'be taken by surprise', 'be caught unawares' is especially appropriate here.

For exclusion from the synagogue, see commentary on 9:22. The 'killing' (2) may refer to the Jewish penalty for blasphemy (5:18; 10:33), or the pagan lynching for insult to local deities (Acts 14:11–19). The spiritual blindness described in 16:2 is among the greatest tragedies that have recurred throughout religious history (see Acts 22:3–5; 26:9–11).

'Their hour' (4) has in it a hint of hope as well as realism. The world will have its limited opportunity of persecution; they must expect it as he expected his hour of suffering and death. But the hour would pass, and beyond it lay a time when the world's hatred would be powerless, and the 'ruler of this world' be judged (16:11).

Suggestions for group discussion:

1   What does the group consider the most important lesson of the vine, for each Christian, and for the Church? Is our 'resignation' from Christian work ever God's 'pruning'?
2   This passage expresses an ambivalent attitude towards the world: expecting relentless hostility, yet witnessing with a view to its conversion. This raises awkward questions about world-Church relationships. Should we emphasize the distinction more that we usually do? Should a Christian contribute to, hold aloof from, or condemn, the world's culture, art, science, politics, ambitions? Can we influence the world without identifying with it? Should evangelists imitate the world's expertise, advertising, motives of appeal?

Three further footnotes   *John 16:5–33*

First footnote

The exciting promise of the Spirit, mentioned in 14:16–18, 26; 15:26, is here extended in face of two specific needs, the awful vacuum that will be left by Jesus' departure, and the disciples' unreadiness to face the unpredictable future. Both needs were touched upon, as the Holy Spirit (Jesus' 'other self') was introduced; now the disciples' consternation at Jesus' going is met with the assurance that it will prove an advantage. The Counsellor cannot come unless Jesus goes (7; compare 7:39), and his ministry will be closer, and unending. The Spirit's coming, Jesus' sending, and Jesus' coming (14:18) are equivalent phrases.

Jesus is drawing his instructions to a close with words he could not have spoken earlier, when he spent the days with them: now his leaving them is very near. Yet 5 (at least) must have been spoken before 13:36 and 14:5, perhaps following 13:33. However that may be, 16:6–7 (or 6–11) certainly sets the shock of 13:33 into a different context, as a positive good, since by going Jesus will 'make way' (so to speak) for the Spirit who will replace him (14:16), and bear clear witness to Christ to them, in them and through them.

Now (8–11) Jesus adds that the Spirit will act as prosecuting counsel, bringing the world to conviction about the enormity of sin, the true nature of righteousness, and the certainty of judgment. The world's crucial sin, in John's eyes, was the unbelief that cut it off from God and from eternal life. The true nature of righteousness (much discussed by Jews and Greeks) had been shown in Jesus' life and teaching, upon which God would set the approving seal of Christ's ascension (10). The certainty of judgment would be evident as Jesus' clash with the ruler of this world left Satan humiliated, Jesus vindicated. Jesus' presence in the world had exposed evil in searching light; as John had lived to see, the Spirit through the Church would perpetuate also this side of Christ's message and ministry.

The second need, the disciples' unreadiness for the future, was deepened by their inability to receive all Jesus had to say. The time was short, the mood was wrong, and some lessons only experience and reflection would make clear. But the Spirit of truth would guide them into all they needed to know amid the new problems and confused issues of the coming years.

The disciples (and the Church after them) need not fear some new revelation contradicting their experience of Jesus. The Spirit will not speak on his own initiative or authority; he will declare what is given to him explaining, exploring, and expanding 'the unsearchable riches of Christ'. The first function of the Spirit will be to glorify Christ (12–15).

He will also lead them into the uncharted future, showing things to come and doubtless guiding Christian reaction to them. As Jesus spoke, 'things to come' included the cross and the resurrection; as John wrote, they included all the intervening years of change and growth, and, still ahead, the promised advent.

Of course, this is no promise of infallibility, of encyclopedic knowledge, or theological acumen. As all that is the Father's is given to the Son (15; 13:3), so the Spirit will take what belongs to the Son and share it with the disciples, as circumstances make necessary and spiritual insight makes possible. Thus is promised a perpetually enriching, open-ended, adventurous spiritual education for the humblest of believers. The proud, who know everything already, miss it!

In both respects, therefore, the Spirit, as the form of the contemporary Christ in each generation, will prolong the ministry of the departing Jesus in the ongoing Church.

Second footnote

The theme changes abruptly: we hear no more about the Spirit, but are back with the puzzled disciples and their questions. The reiterated 'a little while . . . we do not know what he means . . .' vividly describes their bewilderment. When this discussion arose is not clear, but 14:19 could have provoked it (16–18).

Jesus refers, almost certainly, to the 'little while' before his death, when the disciples would sorrow and the world rejoice (20), and to the subsequent 'little while' that would bring his resurrection and ascension, when the disciples' sorrow would turn into joy (22). The immediate future held its dangers, but to hearts sure that Jesus had ascended, it could certainly be said 'no one will take your joy from you'. Joy occurs, in these closing lines, on that awful night, five times!

In this context, the metaphor of a woman in travail means simply that the 'little while' of distress would be limited, as at a birth, and issue in permanent joy. To that assurance are added, rather abruptly, sayings about 'asking'. In that day (23, 26) can refer only to the end of the little while; by that time all that puzzled them now will be clarified. They need not then ask about anything.

But they will still ask for things. A richer prayer experience will be one of their chief gains in their life between the advents (see commentary on 14:13; 15:16). Just when the disciples fear that the excitement and enrichment of their time with Jesus is coming to an end, Jesus promises a fellowship more intimate, enriching, and enduring, than anything they have known. Their joy will be full (23–24).

Jesus' immediate meaning is thus clear. But why did John record so laboriously a conversation whose relevance was perhaps fifty years out of date? What bewildered the disciples in the Upper Room had long been clarified by events. And why does John repeat 'a little while' seven times?

We can only guess, carefully, but two clues may help us. One is that figure of the woman in travail, which from Isaiah (13:6–9; 26:16–21) and Jeremiah (4:28–31), from the rabbinic doctrine of the travail-woes which would herald the messianic age, to Paul (Romans 8:22–25; 1 Thessalonians 5:2–3) and Revelation (12:1–6), had been associated with the coming of the Lord, the Day of the Lord, and divine judgment. Jesus, too, so used the figure, in Mark 13:8 (NIV). By John's time, it was accepted advent-language.

The other clue is the Church's bewilderment, towards the end of the first century, about the promise of Christ's return. For two generations Christians had looked for the imminent return of Christ, recalling such sayings as Mark 9:1, sometimes neglecting their daily work in advent excitement, sometimes worried about friends who had died too soon, and even advised that there was not really time to enter into marriage (see 1 Thessalonians 4:10–18; 5:1–12; 2 Thessalonians 3:6–13; 1 Corinthians 7:26–31).

But Jesus had not come. The promised 'little while' between seeing him and seeing him again had stretched into decades. Various explanations were offered: Jesus had warned of delay (Matthew 24:36–44, 48; 25:5, 19); the advent had already occurred (2 Thessalonians 2:1–10); God's timing is different from ours (2 Peter 3:4, 8–10).

John's answer to the whispering he heard about him in the churches ('What does a little while really mean? When will the Lord come?') may be to recall the similar questioning in the Upper Room, and the metaphor of the woman in travail that Jesus then used. They were troubled, then, too, about Jesus' 'little while' (John seems to say), and Jesus used our advent-language to assure them that every such waiting time is limited, its length is known, and joy shall reward a patient faith. Certainly John did expect the return of Christ. Beside his emphasis upon Christ's presence with us as the Spirit, John sets the expectation that God's purposes for the world have a climax and a culmination. Jesus will come (14:3, 8; compare 1 John 3:2); he twice echoes the eucharistic hope 'till he come' (21:22-23); there is to be a 'last day' of resurrection and judgment (5:28–29; 6:39–54, and so on). Jesus' enemies have their hour, but in God's good time Jesus will be glorified.

However difficult to imagine such an advent may be—and John says nothing of clouds, angels, trumpets, nor of flaming wrath—yet a purposive universe must have a goal, and Christian faith must nourish a hope, and one in which Jesus has a place. God is neither amusing himself nor wasting 'time': his will shall finally be done, and Christ is his agent. Many modern Christians are more sure of the presence now of the Spirit of Christ than they are of his coming; a few are more sure of his promised coming than aware that he is here. John's message about the future is that Christ is with us in the Spirit and coming in greater glory. To lack either aspect of faith is to be poorer Christians than need be.

Third footnote

Verses 25–33 are full of echoes of the conversation as given at chapter 14 (26 echoes 14:13–14; 27 echoes 14:21; 28 echoes 14:12, 28; 33 echoes 14:27, 30). Its appropriateness as a closing paragraph, parallel to chapter 14, is obvious. But to what figures concerning the Father does 25 refer? Not to the figure of the vine, or the travailing woman; could the reference be to 'the Father's house', or to some part of the conversation never preserved? There is good authority for translating 'figure' (25) as 'dark, bewildering saying'—which suits the context well. He will say nothing more to bewilder them, but speak plainly.

The purpose of these verses is to describe the disciples' immediate position, and the faith in which Jesus faces death. As Jesus has assured them so often, they will be able henceforth to pray in his name (26, 23–24; 14:13–14; 15:16), their requests thus being virtually his own. They have the added assurance that the Father himself loves them—for loving Jesus. So Jesus need not beg the Father either to answer or to love them: they will have access to the Father for themselves (compare Romans 5:2; Ephesians 2:18; Hebrews 4:16).

Verse 26 does not preclude Jesus' continued intercession (Romans 8:34; Hebrews 7:25), but Christ's mediation does not keep God at a distance, nor does it persuade God to love—for that there is no need. Jesus acknowledges that the disciples love and believe (27); he no longer warns against defection, but in the plainest terms states his origin and destination in God (28). The disciples reply with an equally plain declaration of their faith (30). The verse reads oddly, but probably means that Jesus knows their thoughts before they question him; Christ's insight into others' minds has been emphasized throughout the Gospel (see 1:47–49). Jesus does not question their faith, but solemnly and sadly warns of the test to come (Mark 14:27; John 16:1).

In response to the disciples' faith, Jesus states as plainly the faith in which he faces death:

'I am not alone': The disciples' temporary scattering may be painful, but Jesus knows still the Father's sustaining presence. John might almost be correcting any wrong impression left by Jesus' reciting Psalm 22 upon the cross, 'My God, my God, why hast thou forsaken me?' Or recalling 'He who sent me is with me; he has not left me alone' (8:29). The calm serenity of the very last moment has begun already as they leave the Upper Room, preparing for that prayer of infinite peace, 'Father, into thy hands...'

'In me you may have peace': Living as they will be, in two environments simultaneously, in the world and in Christ, the disciples may well know both tribulation and tranquillity (33, see commentary on 14:27). At that moment Jesus' words have special poignancy and power. He alone knew just what 'tribulation' was being prepared for him but his resolve was unshaken, his heart strong. In so far as the disciples' lives also were centred upon God, they could share that unfathomable peace.

'I have overcome the world': for peace could rise to cheerfulness (33), a trumpet-note to close upon! The hostility that awaits them is but the fury of a foe who senses defeat. In crucifying Jesus evil would overreach itself. The 'ruler of this world' being judged, and the world itself convicted of sin, righteousness and judgment, Jesus has only to wait. All his humiliation will be eclipsed in triumph and glory—let the disciples, then, be of good cheer!

So the sad evening closes on a note of peace and hope. The Father's presence, unassailable peace, and assured victory over evil, wove that triple armour in which Jesus went forth from the Upper Room to die. But first, he prayed.

Suggestions for group discussion:

1   John's record of Jesus' promise of the Spirit mentions exclusively intellectual gifts of memory, understanding, truth, progress, preparation for change, never referring to gifts of healing, ecstatic tongues, prophecy, and the like. In our time these intellectual gifts of the Spirit seem least emphasized or desired. What does the group think?

2   It has been said that in 16:13 'John's Gospel registers an eternal protest against all fixity and settlement of dogma in the Church.' Is this true?

The Lord's prayer   *John 17:1–26*

Self-manifestation is never more complete than when prayer is shared with one's closest circle. Here Jesus opens his very heart, not only to the Father but to the Eleven.

One would not expect a logical structure in earnest praying, but it is possible to trace the movement of Christ's thought. Jesus considers his life's mission, asking that it may be consummated in glory. He prays for the Eleven, and the dangers and tasks ahead of them. And then his intercession widens to include the Church that is to be.

It is the Lord's prayer, not ours. Its assumptions are his alone—'As we are one ... Even as thou art in me and I in thee ... The glory I had with thee ...' Here the complete unity of Father and Son becomes articulate. Nevertheless Jesus prays, the servant still.

Besides, this prayer contains no expression of penitence, no plea for forgiveness, no request for help, or for his own deliverance from evil, no petition for grace. Certainly, then it is no model for ourselves. Whether 24 be translated 'I will' (AV, RV), 'I desire' (RSV, NEB), or 'I want' (NIV), (all are possible renderings), it still breathes a firmer tone than mature Christians would venture to use in prayer.

Yet some things we can learn from Christ's prayer for our own prayer experience. The varied address to God as 'Father', 'holy Father', 'righteous Father', reminds us that all true prayer rests upon the rich character of God; as we think of all he is, so our requests grow larger and more reverent. At the same time our prayer-life becomes more disciplined, for one cannot ask a holy, righteous, loving Father for anything vengeful, unclean, selfish, trivial, nor anything at all that would be hurtful to others, or to oneself.

In Jesus' prayer, intercession for others far outweighs the single request for himself, and that (1, 5) is clearly intended to enhance and share the glory of the Father. In all true prayer, the divine will is paramount; we do not seek to alter God's will; we need not try to persuade God to be wise or loving. All Christian prayer begins 'thy glory... thy will...' and ends, as with Jesus, 'thine is... the glory'.

Equally clearly, for Jesus and for us, prayer is rooted in relationship. This distinguishes Christian prayer from all spells, magic, ritual incantation; it is conversation with one who knows and loves, about what concerns him and ourselves. Its foundation therefore lies in knowledge of each other, and its chief outcome is our acceptance of God's will and his enabling us for it.

First (1–5) Jesus lifts to God in prayer his own life-work and mission in dedication, for acceptance and approval. Throughout, Jesus' accent is that of the servant (4, 6, 8, 14, 22, 26). He has glorified God in all that he has said and done; now, in principle, an hour before his arrest, his work is 'accomplished' (4), and he offers it, with himself, in consecration (19).

The long-awaited hour has come (2:4; 7:6, and so on). The 'career' that began in glory is soon to end, via death and ascension, in glory again, enhancing God's glory. 'Power' (2) is literally authority, in this context authority to bestow eternal life. Verse 3 seems a parenthetical comment, perhaps introduced during public reading (compare 11:2). With 'the only true God', compare 1 John 5:20.

Jesus then lifts to God in prayer his remaining disciples. Judas is remembered, and one can fancy a note of sadness, even regret (12). 'Son of ...' is a familiar Hebrew phrase of description (see 8:44; 12:36; Acts 4:36); it does not carry the implication that Judas was 'born to perdition'. Jesus does not pray for the world (9); there are things you cannot ask for unbelievers (1 John 5:16). In that evening's shadowed atmosphere it must have meant so very much to the Eleven to hear themselves singled out from all others in their master's intercession.

And to note how Jesus described them. They are, six times, God's gift to his Son, having first belonged to God (6, 9, 10). That breathes affection, responsibility, even something of pride in possessing them! Beside, they have learned God's name, nature, and character as they never knew it before (6, 26); they have become convinced that God sent Jesus, which makes them colleagues in his mission (7–8, 25). And they have kept his, and God's word (6, 8, 14).

Nothing is here said about the disciples' 'saintliness' or special qualifications, because these men are not Christ's by their own deserving, but by his choice—privileged, not rewarded (15:16). Yet Jesus can say he is glorified in them (10; in the change wrought in

137

them?). They will bring others (20); they have even shared something of his own glory (22), perhaps by glimpsing in him a glory never previously imagined (1:14; 2:11). And they are loved by the Father, as even the world can see (23, 26).

These are inspiring things to have said of oneself. Equally striking are the parallels which Jesus draws between the disciples and himself:

▷ *that they may be one, even as we are one*

▷ *my joy ... in themselves*

▷ *they are not of the world even as I am not ...*

▷ *as thou didst send me ... so have I sent them*

▷ *I consecrate myself, that they also may be consecrated*

▷ *Thou hast loved them even as thou hast loved me*

▷ *that they may be with me where I am*

▷ *I have given them the words thou gavest me*

▷ *the glory which thou has given me I have given to them.*

Such a remarkable and many-sided identification of the master with his men must have lingered long in the disciples' memories, giving inexhaustible meaning to the 'mutual indwelling' of which Jesus had spoken (14:20).

What Jesus asks for his men also commands attention. 'Father ... keep them ... I kept them ... I have guarded them ... But now I am coming to thee ... Keep them from the evil [one] ...' Jesus knew his men, slow to learn, sometimes dull of understanding, and on occasion quarrelsome. He knew how Thomas would find it hard to keep his faith, though heart-loyal (11:16). He knew that Peter would find it hard to conquer his impulsiveness and fears.

He knew too how the world would hate them, yet their work lay within the world, and they could not be taken out of it (15, 18), so he prayed, repeatedly and earnestly, 'Father, keep them ...' That, too, would be a fortifying memory.

Jesus also asks, repeatedly, 'that they all may be one ... perfectly one' (11, 21–23). The master's mind reverts to the urgency of his new commandment of mutual loyalty. He desires too that his men may share in the fellowship of the Father and the Son ('one ... as we are'). So the world, impressed by the loyalty of Christians to each other, would recognize its source in their years with Jesus, and in the love of God himself for them (23; 13:35).

Thus the beginning and ending of that solemn evening came together in the thought of unbreakable unity in Christ. It is both an obligation, as a command of Christ, and a gift from God to pray for and accept. Without both human resolve and divine help, the Church will never find, or keep, her unity.

The prayer that the Eleven may be 'sanctified in the truth' as he himself is sanctified (17, 19, same Greek word), probably asks that they shall be set apart, made fit and commissioned for the task assigned to them (18). The request that they might come to be with him at the last (20; 14:3) has within it the suggestion that having shared his humiliation and followed him when in eclipse, they may also see his glory and the fulfilment of his mission. So the joy which he asks for them on earth (13) will be completed in glory.

And then—Jesus prays for us, for the continuing Church reaching down the coming generations, united in a chain of witness-kindling-faith to the end of time (20). The burden of that prayer is single and simple: that they, too, may all be one. Such is Jesus' one, and final, prayer for his historic Church. No divided Church can reconcile a divided world, nor heal its hurts, nor sweeten its common life. Too often religious strife has added further bitterness to the world's innumerable divisions.

Has this prayer for unity like that between Father and Son anything at all to do with organizational uniformity, or unvarying practice? Certainly it has everything to do with the inner, spiritual, moral and social unity of Christians, despite whatever variety of emphasis, liturgy and ethos, differences of time and culture may create. The apostolic Church was one amid great variety of worship, organization, background and emphasis. But the variety may endanger the unity, if it be not zealously safeguarded and deliberately fostered. Jesus prayed it might be so, on the very night on which he was betrayed, and beneath the very shadow of his cross.

All in all, a wonderful prayer! 'Lord, teach us to pray.'

Suggestions for group discussion:

1   Does the group agree that the unity the master prayed for has nothing to do with organization or uniformity of practice? What kind of unity should the modern Church be seeking?

2   Christ's final preparation and instruction for the future has assumed that the Church will be there, the Spirit will be there, and he himself will be there. What would the group emphasize as our chief duty towards each of these? And would the group suggest any other vital factor necessary to the modern Church, and the Church of the future—the New Testament? Sacraments? The ministry? Or what?

5

Christ's Self-manifestation in Death and Resurrection

John 18:1—20:31

For the story of the passion, John relies mainly on simple narrative, letting the facts speak for themselves, with only rare comments. His greatest insistence is that nothing that occurred was accidental, all was foreseen (nine references). And the initiative lay always with Jesus. He strode forward to meet the end, himself choosing the place of his arrest (1–2) and its terms (8), and always remaining clearly in command (again mentioned nine times).

As the first Christian sermon revealed (Acts 2), this change of perspective was the first revision of the disciples' attitude towards the death of Jesus. It was no longer a tragedy, a failure, or merely human wickedness triumphing over good; it was something foretold, accepted, and accomplished, a part of Christ's mission. Those who, for their own wilful reasons, brought about Christ's death would bear their own guilt, but they served purposes beyond their knowing. God would weave their actions into his own redemption plan.

A new element enters the story, without explanation, in the person of Pilate, governor of the Roman province of Syria-Palestine. Because of the crowds, and religious and nationalist excitement, at Passover, the governor moved from his headquarters at Caesarea to the Praetorium barracks at Jerusalem, with an increased security guard. This limited the freedom of the Jewish authorities, but they were equally anxious to avoid demonstrations, protests, or other provocation which might endanger the delicate concordat between Jewry and Rome.

The 'trial' of Jesus   *John 18:1—19:16*

Though John does not describe Christ's agony in Gethsemane, he evidently knew of it (1, 11). The suggestion that John was 'unwilling to expose Christ's moment of weakness' scarcely accords with his emphasis upon Christ's dependence and subservience. John did not need to repeat a familiar story which would add nothing to his argument.

Judas betrayed only where Jesus could be arrested secretly and by night, avoiding interference by the people (2–3). The soldiers may have been temple guards, possibly augmented by Romans seconded for Passover duties; Roman officers would normally take any trouble-maker direct to Pilate. They came with lanterns and torches seeking the light of the world! The soldiers' recoil, stumbling against one another in the darkness, probably registers their surprise at Jesus' bold courage (4–6); they expected a cringing fugitive. The later criticism, that Jesus attempted ignominious escape, is being answered by John in 2, 4–8. To the end Jesus protected his own (9; 17:12); 8–9, 15 imply that the disciples accepted the hint and fled.

Peter's reaction (10) was impetuous and loyal, but wrong, and for Jesus exceedingly dangerous if reported to the governor, as perhaps it was (36). Only John reveals the servant's name, his kinsman (26), and who struck him. Curiously, John does not mention that Jesus healed the man (Luke 22:51).

John says that Jesus was taken, bound, to Annas, described as High Priest (15, 19, 22; possibly a courtesy title for the ex-High Priest, defiantly used in protest against Rome's deposing him). Then, at 34, Jesus is taken to Caiaphas, 'High Priest that year' (13, 24; 'that year' probably means 'that important, fateful year'; the office was not an annual appointment). John seems to imply that both were High Priest simultaneously. In addition, he represents Peter as denying Christ in the house of Annas (15–17), and again in the house of Caiaphas (25–27), still warming himself. Yet 'they' (25) appears to mean the servants in Annas' house. Matthew-Mark-Luke say nothing of Annas.

Some early copyists rearranged 13–27 in various ways trying to clarify the story. NEB notes that some manuscript copies place 24 after 13, and a number of scholars accept this. The Jewish trial, and Peter's denial, then took place in the house of Caiaphas, as the other Gospels record. It is a speculative emendation, but such displacements of short phrases did occur—omitted by mistake and then reinserted in the wrong place.

At 14 John recalls Caiaphas' earlier counsel about Jesus (11:49–51), as if to suggest that Jesus was not likely to get a fair hearing before him. 'Another disciple' (15) remains unidentified after much discussion; was he Nicodemus (recall 3:1; 7:50; note 19:39)? Or 'the beloved disciple'? (See our introductory paragraphs 'Why doubt the tradition?') Verses 17–18, 26, show familiarity with the household: the story is told from the point of view of the servants' hall.

Jerusalem, 2,500 feet high, would be cold at dawn in early spring

(18). The question put to Peter, 'You are not one of this man's disciples are you?' (17, 25, as Greek, NIV) by its form invited denial. The Greek and RSV have 'you also', implying 'beside the one we know'. Verse 27 has almost sardonic brevity, as though echoing 13:38.

The questioning of Jesus before Caiaphas was informal, ignoring legal requirement; hence the illegal slap (22), incriminating questions (19), trial during darkness (28). In 20–21 and 23 Jesus requires that his examiners take the evidence properly, from corroborating witnesses, if they can. Some Greek readers would recall that Socrates replied to his judges in similar terms. The question about 'disciples' arose probably from a suspicion of conspiracy. Nothing is here said about a claim to be Messiah, or about blasphemy; the rulers were obsessed with political dangers (11:48–50). No explicit charge is made—another legal informality. A verdict involving death could be given only by Pilate.

The praetorium was Roman headquarters wherever Roman troops were stationed (28). Defilement would arise (28) from any house whence leaven had not, at Passover, been rigorously excluded, (see 1 Corinthians 5:6–8). Gentile premises would be especially 'unclean'. Pilate therefore goes 'out' to the Jews. John leaves readers to notice for themselves the irony of having scruples about ritual uncleanness while plotting murder.

Still the Jews refuse to name a charge, hoping that Pilate will confirm their sentence without close enquiry (30). Not wishing to become their tool, Pilate suggests they settle their own religious squabbles; but that would preclude the death penalty which the Jewish leaders desired. Some find the Jewish attitude incredibly insolent before a Roman governor. It is no more daring than 19:12; the Jews knew that Pilate feared their malicious reporting to Caesar. Verse 32 distinguishes Roman execution by crucifixion from Jewish stoning.

To the Jews' chagrin, Pilate 'calls' Jesus' case into his own hands, privately (33). He questions Jesus on the only subject Rome cared about, though no accusation of sedition had been mentioned. It is hinted at, only, in 19:12. The meaning of 'king' (34, 37) depends upon who uses the word, and how. If Pilate has chosen that word it will imply sedition; then such a question invites self-incrimination. If others have accused Jesus of making that claim, they should be produced and cross-examined.

Pilate evades this challenge with something of impatience, perhaps of contempt (33, 35, 38). He will not bandy words with a village carpenter, but demands to know what action has brought Jesus to arraignment. Jesus replies by defining his 'field of action', a sphere of 'kingship' which cannot incur Rome's condemnation, since it does not rival this world's powers, nor involve fighting (35–36).

Pilate's reaction is incredulous surprise at a confession which is also a claim (37). Jesus further clarifies his position. 'King' was Pilate's word; Jesus prefers to say that he was born to witness to the truth; all who love truth (Jesus implies) acknowledge in him an authority above that of kings (37).

The governor's famous reply (38) can be understood as contemptuous, dismissive, wistful, sceptical, or merely the typical impatience of a practical Roman official with all abstract philosophical questions. His action shows him to be convinced that Jesus' 'offence' is beyond Rome's jurisdiction. Jesus is innocent of any crime. Pilate repeats this at 19:4, 6, and thereafter seeks to evade the Jews' demand that Jesus should die.

First, he offers the customary Passover amnesty. Some find such a custom incredible; others cite instances from early writers; the Jews had certainly wrested many religious privileges from Rome as the price of compromise. The terms of Pilate's offer are again contemptuous, and its content fraudulent, since Jesus had not been convicted. The Jews' call for release of 'the Barabbas' (in Greek, 'the notorious Barabbas') was no less hypocritical, since Barabbas had in fact committed the very offence of which they accused Jesus (19:12; Luke 23:19).

Pilate next offered a compromise, not death but a savage scourging (19:1). In Acts 22:24 an examination by scourging is mentioned, but in Jesus' case the intention appears to be to satisfy Jewish animosity halfway, and most unjustly. The soldiers add a form of horseplay which mocks the supposed claim to kingship: the 'imperial' purple robe, and the 'crown' of thorns. (Philo describes a similar scene taking place at Alexandria.)

Pilate then repeated his declared verdict, Jesus was innocent; and he appealed to the crowd's compassion—'Look at him!' When this failed, exasperated, Pilate told the Jews to take responsibility, asserting yet again that Jesus was innocent (19:4–7). This time the Jews appealed to their religious law concerning blasphemy. Pilate feared this, partly because every governor had learned to handle Jewish religious questions very carefully (see Acts 18:12–17); and partly because like many Roman officials, Pilate was highly superstitious concerning omens or dreams (see Matthew 27:19). He therefore questioned Jesus again, particularly about his origin. In Luke's account this enquiry concerns the area to which Jesus belonged, though in John's record it sounds like a theological enquiry.

After a threefold judicial decision that Jesus was innocent, Pilate should certainly have released Jesus. Further questioning was insincere, mere prevarication. Jesus therefore refused to answer (9; note

Isaiah 53:7). When Pilate resorted to bullying threats of enforced authority, Jesus reminded him of an authority still greater, by implication one to which Pilate himself shall eventually answer (10–11).

Who delivered Jesus to Pilate is not clear: Jesus could mean Judas, the Jews, or (probably) Caiaphas. Whoever was meant, Jesus warns that all human authority derives ultimately from God (the Hebrew doctrine of theocracy; Romans 13:1–4). This makes any misuse of 'human' authority not only a social crime but also a sin answerable to God. In John's time, such an idea would carry warning to persecutors, comfort to the persecuted.

So it sounded to Pilate, who now strove to release Jesus. But the Jews resorted to their last argument, blackmail. Pilate had already earned a reputation for ruthlessness and injustice (see Luke 13:1); he was to be deposed in disgrace only a few years later. He could not, therefore, rely with any confidence upon Caesar's support if Jewish leaders laid information against him, especially in the terms implied in 12. Pilate surrendered, with very bad grace (13, 22).

A curious ambiguity besets 13. Acts 25:6, 17 shows a judge taking his seat on the tribunal to open a trial. If this is what John implies, then all the questioning so far has been preliminary. The trial itself, in that case, was reduced to a mere appeal to the people as jury (13–16).

There is, however, some grammatical authority for thinking that Pilate sat Jesus on the judgment seat, still wearing the purple robe and the mocking crown, and urged the people, contemptuously, to gaze upon their poor, bleeding, exhausted 'king'. Some say such an act was beneath a Roman governor's dignity; but by this time Pilate had little dignity left. He was exasperated, outwitted, humiliated, and very, very angry, a man quite capable of taking rude revenge.

Once more in John we come upon truth spoken by accident (recall 11:50–51). The official representative of the greatest empire in history, speaking juridically in Caesar's name, declares of Jesus of Nazareth 'Here is your king!' He is answered by the insensate cry of an hysterical, vengeful crowd, concerned now not with all that Jesus had said and done, but only with the endless tug-of-war between Jewish and Roman authority. Pilate tries once more, and this time his contempt stings the Jewish leaders to the ironic, and to the Jews blasphemous, declaration, 'We have no king but Caesar!' No wonder the exact place, day and time of those two declarations were precisely recorded! (14–15).

Having wrung that disastrous confession from the leaders of the most rebellious nation within the empire, and to save his own place and reputation, Pilate helplessly 'yielded him to them' (16, Greek), though only Roman soldiers could perform the execution.

Throughout, Jesus stands in sharpest contrast with the Roman governor, in character, in self-command, in integrity, in authority. There is no doubt which emerged unscathed from this confrontation, first with Caiaphas and then with Pilate. Nor any doubt where real, enduring power lay. To this day, right across the world, millions acclaim Jesus 'Lord', and remember that he 'suffered under Pontius Pilate . . . was crucified . . . [and] rose again'.

It was important to John's thought of Jesus as a Passover sacrifice that he should be repeatedly declared 'unblemished', by the absence of any sustainable accusation, and by the verdicts not only of those who loved and knew him best but also by the highest authority in the contemporary world. It is John's achievement to have shown Jesus accused, 'tried', ultimately condemned to die, yet peerless, unstained, unyielding before evil, unafraid to the last, truly 'the lamb of God'.

Suggestions for group discussion:

1   It has been argued that Pilate's triple declaration of Jesus' innocence affirms that Christianity itself is 'politically innocent', in the sense of being totally detached from political affairs. Is this true? Should it be true in the modern world?
2   Of the various people who shared in bringing about the death of Jesus—Judas, the Sanhedrin, Caiaphas, the crowd, Pilate, the soldiers—who, in the group's opinion, bears most of the blame? Would the group attempt to place them in order of culpability?

The death of Jesus   *John 19:17–42*

John's skill at simple yet powerful narration is nowhere better shown than in these twenty-six verses. His insistence that Jesus bore 'his own' cross seems directed against a Gnostic idea that Simon of Cyrene bore it, and died instead of Christ 'since God cannot suffer' (compare Luke 23:26).

'Golgotha' is Aramaic for 'skull' (and in Latin gives us 'Calvary'); it may refer to the shape of the hill at that time. It was not 'a place of skulls', which Jews would not tolerate; Origen's suggestion, that Adam was buried nearby, was Christian fancy.

In death, Jesus is 'numbered with transgressors' (Isaiah 53:12), yet proclaimed in Palestine's three languages 'King of the Jews', which taunted the Jews, amused Pilate and expressed his stubbornness, but would be recognized by all Christian readers to be literal truth, fulfilling Scripture. In dealing with the prisoner's clothes, likewise, the soldiers unconsciously fulfilled Psalm 22:18. John loves these ironic touches!

The quaternion of soldiers (23) was matched (probably, but no one can be sure) by four women of faith (25). 'Magdalene' means 'of

Magdala', a village three miles from Capernaum, notorious for its wealth and its immorality, according to the Talmud. Jesus' care of his mother is not a symbol; he loved the one who bore and nourished him, and who now grieves for him. 'I thirst' registers Jesus' intense suffering, now reaching exhaustion; it also echoes Psalm 22:15. John is narrating facts, not listing clues to mystic meanings. On 'the beloved disciple' (26) see our introductory paragraphs, 'Why doubt the tradition?' and the reference there to this incident.

Verse 28 probably passes over a long interval of darkness and silence. Death by crucifixion could take two or three days, though probably not when following scourging. The cheap wine of the common soldier was different from the drugged wine which charitable women offered to criminals to ease their end.

'It is finished' (30) is a cry of accomplishment; the divine mission was fulfilled. Jesus had attained a total, willing obedience (10:18) without once descending to the level of the forces ranged against him. The cry was therefore also a cry of victory. At that moment, again in perfect self-command, Jesus 'gave up' his spirit (John's phrase resembles the Greek of Isaiah 53:12 'poured out his soul').

The sabbath that began that evening was doubly sacred as Passover sabbath. Jewish Law forbade the exposure of the bodies of those executed (Deuteronomy 12:23), especially over such a day. That it was not necessary to break Jesus' legs to hasten death seemed, to Christian piety, to accord with Psalm 34:20, as the piercing of Christ's side 'fulfilled' Zechariah 12:10. The soldiers' action seems quite purposeless, unless to make sure Jesus died. It is possible that John has in mind some who 'explained' the empty tomb by arguing that Jesus swooned, but did not die.

'Medical explanations' of the result (34) have convinced few. But John saw some great significance in the incident, since he insists so strongly on the truth of his record, and adds someone else's confirming testimony. ('His testimony is true, and he knows that he tells the truth' would be a very clumsy way of saying 'my testimony . . . I know . . . I tell'; someone else is confirming what 'he who saw it' said; compare 21:24.) Here again John may have in mind certain Gnostic theories, mentioned by Irenaeus (roughly AD130–202), that Jesus, not being a real man, did not bleed (note 1 John 5:6).

Another explanation would link 34–35 with the three perpetual witnesses to Christ's redemptive work which exist in the ongoing life of the Church, namely the Spirit, baptism, and eucharist (1 John 5:6–8; the terms used are unexpected, but no other interpretation is plausible). In 34–35 John may be suggesting that the water of baptism and the 'blood' of the eucharist, which constantly cleanse Christian converts through the Church's ministry, derive from the actual moment of Christ's death for them upon the cross. Later, John will likewise suggest that the presence in the life of the Church of the third 'witness', the Spirit, derives from the action of the risen Christ on Easter Day (20:22).

Such an argument would have importance in John's day. The Christian sacraments, he would say, are no magical or mystical wonders, as the baptisms and sacred meals of the mystery religions were held to be. They were simply the application to individual believers, to the end of time, of what Jesus obtained for them by his literal and historical death upon Golgotha.

It must be confessed that such an interpretation does not lie upon the surface of 34–35, hence the tentative manner of the comment offered. But John's readers would be familiar with rival 'sacramental' ideas; and 1 John 5 lends this interpretation considerable support. Such an understanding of the incident would also explain the strong emphasis John has laid upon the truth of his record.

Once again Christian reflection has discovered scriptural phrases which 'portend' the details of the story (36–37); and once again an event concerning Jesus leads on to faith. Two hesitant followers now declare themselves openly as on Jesus' side, belatedly, but in the circumstances very bravely. Mark says Joseph 'plucked up courage' (Mark 15:43).

As a member of the Sanhedrin (Luke 23:50), Joseph of Arimathea (a city in Judea) could ask access to Pilate; the apocryphal Gospel of Peter says he was a friend of Pilate; the tomb was probably intended to be his own. Nicodemus (recall 3:1; 7:50) brought embalming unguent (resinous gum and fragrant wood-powder, compare Psalm 45:8) a hundred times the weight of that used by Mary of Bethany, to the scandal of Judas! The preparations, like the new tomb, were fit for a king.

No poet could have ended the story of Christ's dying with a more perfect cadence of beauty and of peace than John does in 41–42.

Nevertheless John is not concerned merely to tell the story, nor even to tell it well. He has repeatedly emphasized that Jesus' dying was a voluntary act in obedience to the Father, fulfilled through the wickedness of men, certainly, but because faithfulness to his mission, and the redemption of the world, demanded it (10:18; 14:31). He has stressed, too, that all was foreseen, even foretold, giving at least nine instances of scriptural 'fulfilment'. This meant, as every Jewish reader would understand, that all that happened was in line with the divine will and purpose.

Moreover, John has kept the story of Jesus' death closely related to the Passover festival in at least nine details, including the haste involved, the timing, the gathered crowds, the rod of hyssop (29; Exodus 12:22; Leviticus 14:4), Jesus' innocence, and his unbroken ('unblemished') body as an acceptable lamb, and the rest.

In this way John links Jesus' death with the annual total purification which (as he reminds us, 11:55; 18:28) the festival imposed. And also with the essential meaning of that great occasion—the celebration of Israel's redemption from Egyptian slavery into freedom and nation-hood. Christ died, our Passover lamb, bearing the sin of the world, to redeem all into greater freedom still (8:32, 34–36; 10:9–10).

Beside this, John's final interpretation of Christ's death, we must set the other things John said, if we would do justice to all his meaning. He declares that Jesus died:

▷ *as the Servant of the Lord and of men, who would purify all willing to be cleansed, by bearing their iniquities and washing the feet of humanity (13:1–16)*

▷ *as the serpent which Moses raised upon a pole to be the focus of the faith which heals the poisoned hurt of the world (3:14)*

▷ *as the bread of life, his flesh broken to feed the hungry, his blood shed to be drunk by a dying world, to bring nourishment and life to all who believe (6:33, 35, 50–58)*

▷ *as the faithful shepherd, torn by the wolves that threaten the flock, and dying to give them eternal security (10:11–15, 27–29)*

▷ *as corn cast into the soil to shrivel and 'die' in order to bear fruit in other lives (12:24–25)*

▷ *as hero in the agelong fight against evil and for good, achieving victory for God and others by his valiant self-sacrifice (12:31; 16:33)*

▷ *as the magnet of all hearts drawing all men towards himself by the universal attraction of vicarious suffering and selfless love (12:32; 11:51–52)*

▷ *as the true Messiah, of a new kind, that rides upon a donkey, will not fight, and wins his crown by consent of willing hearts, responding to the truth (12:13–15; 18:33, 37; 19:1–3, 14–15, 19)*

▷ *as one exposing and judging the real nature of evil, breaking its fascination over human hearts and destroying the pretence that it is merely negative, 'good out of place', and unimportant (12:31; 14:30)*

▷ **as bestower of the Spirit; who could not come until the Christ was glorified in death and resurrection, and so liberated from one age and one land to serve the whole world in every age (7:39; 16:7)**

▷ **as host within the Father's house, going before to prepare lodging and welcome, and coming again to renew fellowship with his own (14:1–3).**

Simply to place John's statements side by side in this way is to show forcefully the importance which John attached to Christ's death in the accomplishing of human salvation. Especially if we remember that most of these statements are words of Jesus himself. It reveals how deeply John had meditated upon the cross, and how much he shared of the common Christian belief concerning it. For the only allusions peculiar to John on this theme are the serpent, the corn of wheat, and the magnet.

At the same time, John's many-sided interpretation of Jesus' death illustrates well his refusal to be bound to any one definition of what Christ in dying achieved for his own. He seems to delight in showing what Jesus did from every possible angle, and to set that single, final act of his saving ministry in every possible light—as offering some benefit to all sorts and conditions of men and women.

Suggestions for group discussion:

1 Modern Christians frequently minimize, or deny, the deliberate, sacrificial, sin-bearing aspects of Christ's death. Does this make much difference to our thought of Jesus, or to the quality of our Christianity? What alternative view of the meaning of Christ's death would members of the group offer?

2 A publisher declared impatiently that 'modern Christians do not want to hear about [Christ's] death, but about something positive— about life'. Is this true? Is it faithful to the Gospel? If so, what do members of the group usually experience in the service of the Lord's Supper?

Resurrection, and reactions   *John 20:1–31*

True to his immediate purpose (20:31), John tells the great story of Jesus' resurrection through the reactions of those who responded to it with varying degrees of faith. It was the report of Mary that stirred Peter and 'the beloved disciple' (see commentary on 19:26) to visit Jesus' tomb, not some excited anticipation of a miracle, or the hopeful recalling of Jesus' half-understood promises, but the bare news that the Lord's body had been taken and was lost. John knows that someone had accompanied Mary ('we', 2; see Mark 16:1), though he does not say so.

Peter was not with the other disciples, though evidently within reach; the Greek of 2 implies that Mary made two visits, and 10 mentions 'their homes'; Mark 16:7 confirms this. John's account here is too vividly told not to have eyewitness behind it somewhere—the eagerness that did not wait to arrive together; one disciple peering into the tomb but too awed to enter; impetuous Peter charging in, seeing details, then the other disciple gaining boldness, and believing at any rate what he saw; neither man knowing what had happened; or grasping the Scripture promises; both making their way home in sheer bewilderment (2–10)!

No one would have imagined, or could have invented this. The greatest discovery in history is made in this tame, pedestrian fashion. The presence of the shroud and turban would be inexplicable if the body had been stolen. John appears to assume Jesus' body had been changed in some way (14; 21:4; compare Luke 24:16; 1 Corinthians 15:35–53, and 'his glorious body' in Philippians 3:21).

Such was the first reaction to the most wonderful news ever to break upon the world, on that first Christian Sunday morning: bewildered half-belief. Peter saw without comprehending; the beloved disciple saw, part-believed, and pondered. To see the facts, and gradually grasp their meaning, is (so John often implies) precisely how every soul makes its way towards faith (recall 1:39, 46).

The second story, too, is far too lifelike, yet unexpected, to be invention. Mary haunted the only place where knowledge of Jesus might be gained, openly weeping, insisting still upon the one salient point, the loss of Christ's body. The confusion of tears, and the darkness, further delayed recognition until the beloved voice spoke her name—then the instant, one-word leap of recognition, acceptance, belief, and the simple, central certainty never to leave her again, 'I have seen the Lord!' (18).

It is useless to pretend to explain the angel-visitors from beyond: a vision, a later embellishment of the story, literal fact, who can say? Mary shows no fear, no surprise, nor even disappointment at not being allowed to grasp Jesus. With far quicker faith than the men could show, all was accepted as natural, wonderful, and right.

But we are puzzled. Why was Mary forbidden to hold Jesus ('hold on to' NIV; 'cling to' NEB), when Thomas is later invited to touch him? And what is implied by 'for I have not yet ascended to the Father'? It can scarcely mean 'You may hold me afterwards'. Together with the message sent to the brethren, the words appear to mean 'Do not hinder me ... I am about to ascend ...' If that is right, John must have thought that Jesus' initial ascension occurred that same day. The ascension described in Acts 1 would then be Jesus' final appearance and departure. According to John, then, Jesus' rising, initial ascension, coming to the disciples (19) and bestowing the Spirit (22), together comprised that wonderful day of victory, fulfilment, endowment and promise which we call Easter Day.

Of all the millions of Christian believers Mary was the first to understand that world-changing event. She saw, through her tears, far more clearly than the men; she had loyalty and patience to linger for enlightenment; so she learned, almost at once, the difference Christ's resurrection had made. Jesus is now to her more than 'my teacher' (16); he is 'the Lord' (18). And he and his own do not now stand on quite the same level before God, for he speaks of 'my Father and your Father, my God and your God' (17) ('your' being plural each time).

This also Mary accepts without question, and she becomes not only the first to see the risen Christ, the first to understand what has happened, but also the first to testify to the essential Christian experience (18). Adoring love is another sure way to Christian faith.

John's third Easter story concerns the disciple group as a whole. It is curious (and yet again not something invented) that the news of Jesus' resurrection should have reached the disciples so informally, and so late. A day of rumour, separation, sadness, and fear brought them to an evening gathering, uncertain, bewildered, behind locked doors. It is surely poor stagecraft! One might have expected a shining Christ descending upon Olivet, bringing rapture to his friends and overwhelming dread to all his foes. But John tells it as it was.

Jesus came with his customary 'Shalom!' (Peace!), and for credentials showed his wounds. The evening, the situation, their lives, their very world, were all transformed. Sight of him brought relief, enlightenment, gladness, and a deeper, steadier, more lasting 'shalom' (14:22; 16:33). For now the world was right way up again, God was on his throne, and all was well.

At this point the story of the Church begins: the risen Lord in the midst of his people confers his commission, his Spirit, and his authority. The commission is simply to pursue his own mission, received from the Father (21). The breathing upon them of the Spirit fulfilled the promise of another Counsellor to encourage them, bear witness, and convince the world (see commentary on 14:16–20, 26; 16:7–15; 7:39; for the 'breathing' compare Genesis 2:7; Ezekiel 37:9). Verse 22 records a private, individual bestowal of the power that was to be demonstrated publicly at Pentecost (Acts 2:1–21; 4:31); Paul and

Cornelius received such private endowment after Pentecost (Acts 9:17–19; 10:44).

The conferring of authority to forgive sins has been variously understood, from the priestly rite of formal absolution (nowhere practised in Acts) to the preaching of repentance and forgiveness in Christ's name (Luke 24:46–47, and so through Acts), with perhaps the occasional pastoral reassuring of guilt-afflicted individuals. 'Retaining' sins (23) apparently means 'not forgiving', or perhaps firmly declaring divine judgment (Acts 5:3–11; 13:9–11).

We do not know to how many this threefold gift was given on that Easter evening. Paul mentions 'the twelve' (1 Corinthians 15:5); Luke speaks of 'the eleven... and those who were with them' when two more arrived from Emmaus though Thomas (and Judas) were absent (Luke 24:33). Nor is it clear whether the commission, the authority and the Spirit were then given only for those present, or also for their 'successors'—though most would probably agree that the commission and the Spirit were bestowed on the whole continuing Church.

The reaction of that disciple group to the resurrection of Jesus is described in a single word, gladness (20). After the doubt, bewilderment, and fear of that long weekend, that was no insignificant response. Faith can dawn in sudden, joyful revelation of the truth, last a lifetime, and irradiate everything. It is interesting, too, to recognize in the experience of that first Easter evening the elements of Christian worship from earliest days: the Lord's Day gathering, the presence of Christ, the greeting of peace, the vision of Christ crucified, renewed gladness, the words of Christ, recommissioning, the renewal of the Holy Spirit, and the renewal also of forgiveness (in the eucharist).

Though John never uses the word, his Gospel, because of passages like 19–23, has been called the Gospel of the Church. Her continuing existence is assumed in the Upper Room discourse and the prayer that followed, in the way that John and Jesus could speak as from within the Church (1:14, 16; 3:11), in references to the body of Christ (2:21), the vine, and the new commandment, as well as to the fold of God. John has much to say about the Church's worship (chapter 4), her ministry (10:1–16; 15:1–8; 20:22–23; 21:15–17), and her sacraments (1:33; 3:5–8, 26; 4:1–2; 9:11; 13:8–10; 6:51–56; 19:34–35).

John does not record the Lord's commanding baptism or the eucharist, but he does emphasize that a true sacrament must convey what it represents, new life in baptism, continual spiritual nourishment in the eucharist. In general, the ongoing life of the Church is everywhere rooted in the life and teaching of her Lord, her ministry perpetuating his until he comes (21:23).

John's fourth Easter story brings his whole argument to a magnificent climax in the awestruck confession that Jesus is indeed Lord and God. Thomas (introduced at 11:16) had been unaccountably absent on Easter Day. Hearing what the disciples reported, he refused to believe ('I will not') unless he could see and touch Christ's wounds, apparently as credentials for his true identity, or for his physical reality ('see', 'touch' suggests he suspected some hallucination, or pious vision). He is still 'one of the twelve' (24) however, and present a week later, perhaps hoping to be convinced.

Jesus appears, again through locked doors, yet he offers Thomas the sight-and-touch confirmation he demanded, with the significant appeal, 'Do not become faithless...' (so Greek, not 'Do not remain faithless...'). Thomas was uncertain, not cynical ('stop doubting and believe' NIV). We are not told if Thomas accepted Christ's invitation (which suggests he did not): but with awe, worship, and total surrender he breathed the supreme confession 'My Lord and my God!'

That statement of faith was crucial for Christians, far beyond the initial Jewish insight of Nathanael (1:49), and echoing that of the mature evangelist himself (1:1–3). It would also appeal forcibly to many Gentile minds, being common in Egyptian, Hellenist, and Roman writing: Domitian the emperor especially liked to be called 'lord and god'. John never forgets that he is writing for a wide audience.

So far as the record shows, Jesus appeared expressly to meet Thomas' demands, treating with sympathy the indecision and doubt of his cautious but loyal disciple (11:16). Thomas is rewarded with the highest of Christ's sixteen beatitudes (29). This defines the basis of faith for the coming Church, for most of whom, by John's day, literal sight-and-touch knowledge of Jesus was impossible.

Henceforth, though knowledge of Christ will continue to depend upon the recorded testimony of those who did see and touch Jesus (see 1 John 1:1–3), faith in him will consist of individual conviction, reached by the insight of perceptive understanding, and based upon personal confrontation with the living Christ like that of Thomas (compare 1 Peter 1:8). (This distinction between the original belief kindled by sight of Jesus and all subsequent belief kindled by insight, would be still clearer, if the opening words of 29 were taken as a statement, not a question; so NIV, NEB, AV, RV, ASV.)

The reaction of Thomas to the resurrection of Jesus is even more unexpected, even farther beyond imaginative myth-making, than the other three. Thomas brings a pessimistic realism and caution to challenge the testimony of men and women he has lived amongst, with Jesus, and so to question the Christians' central confidence. Yet he finds Jesus sympathetic, welcoming, convincing. The same opportunity to meet Jesus face to face is offered to all John's readers in 30–31. Through the ensuing years, many and many a heart, finding faith hard to hold on to, has blessed Thomas for his honesty.

Verse 29 was John's intended and altogether fitting conclusion. His first 'tail-piece' (30–31) admits that the record is incomplete, and perhaps alludes to other books where other things are written— 'books' meaning, of course, inscribed papyrus rolls. And then he states his purpose in writing, to show who Jesus was and is, that readers might come to possess the life he offers (see our introductory paragraphs, 'What Sort of Book?' for full examination of this crucial statement).

Suggestions for group discussion:

1   John's picture of Jesus is very different from those of Matthew, Mark and Luke. (Recall our introductory paragraphs 'What Has John Done With Jesus' Story?') Does this mean that we all see Jesus in our own way, and no one sees him as he really was?

2   Is there any place in Christian discipleship for doubt like that of Thomas? Is it something to be condemned, as the Church has so often taught? How would the group suggest doubt might be prevented, or cured?

6

Afterthoughts

John 21:1–25

Verses 1–3 are as clearly a new beginning as 20:28–31 were a most appropriate ending. Thomas and Nathanael are introduced again, almost as though we had not already met them; 'the beloved disciple' and the sons of Zebedee we are expected to know without their names; Zebedee, too, as someone already familiar, although he has not previously been mentioned. After the great confession of faith by Thomas, even the moving story of Peter's meeting with the Jesus he had denied has a slight air of anticlimax.

The chapter is certainly precious, but in the overall pattern of the book it is clearly an appendix of 'afterthoughts'.

The restoration of Peter   John 21:1–19

The scene changes to Galilee; Peter is leader again, and with a curious lack of excitement at what has happened, the disciples go fishing as of old. Strangely, too, Peter does not immediately recognize Jesus. Morning mist over the sea probably explains the failure to recognize; and the simple fact that men need to eat, and for fishermen that the sea is the obvious source of supply, explains the fishing. It is needless to imagine deeper motives, such as want of faith, or despair.

Nor is Peter's prominence surprising, if we remember that Jesus appeared to Peter, privately, on Easter Day (Luke 24:34), and Peter was among the Eleven that evening. The personal relationship between Jesus and Peter was evidently re-established, though more was to be required for full spiritual restoration after Peter's denial, which is what John (only) is about to record.

A meeting in Galilee had been prearranged, according to Mark, and was mentioned again by 'the young man' at the tomb (Mark 14:28; 16:7). Its purpose may have been merely to gain quiet and privacy away from the city where the movements of the Eleven would be closely watched. However that may be, its consequence was to take Peter, especially, back to his beginning. For it was beside this sea, after a fruitless night's fishing and an exceptional catch in the morning, that Peter had been called to 'catch men', and had left everything to follow Christ (Luke 5:1–11).

John's story and Luke's are so alike that the question inevitably arises: did the same tradition reach Luke and John in different contexts? The words in Luke's account which puzzle us, 'Depart from me, for I am a sinful man, O Lord', would sound so appropriate after Peter's denial of Christ. But John does not record them; and we must remember those meetings with Jesus on Easter Day. (For the relation of Peter's first interview with Jesus to Luke's story of his call, see commentary on 1:41–42.)

It is at least equally probable that Jesus took opportunity silently to recall to Peter that earlier experience, and the frequent blundering and weakness which had followed, just as the charcoal fire (9, as at 18:18), the threefold 'Do you love me?', the reminder of his boast that though all others forsake Jesus, he never would (15; 13:21), and the repetition of the original call, 'Follow me', all become aids to Peter's memory, and probes to his conscience. Repetition of the fruitless night and morning catch would not be surprising; there would be other occasions when watchers on the shore could see the movement of shoals in the level rays of the rising sun more clearly than men in a boat, looking from above. For neither John nor Luke speak of these catches as 'miracles'.

This reading of the incident is confirmed by Peter's intense grief (17) as he suddenly perceived Jesus' purpose. The outburst, 'Lord, you know everything; you know that I love you', reveals how Peter's heart was wrung as the physician of souls cleansed Peter's guilty memory by a triple avowal of love, cancelling the triple denial. And by the triple renewal of his commission, as pastor of the flock, now, not fisher of men. Weakness, blundering, impetuous actions, can all be dealt with by experience, if Peter loves Christ.

Jesus uses only here the familiar address 'lads' (5); 'stripped for work' meant to a waistcloth (7), and respect for Jesus called for better covering. Much has been made of the one hundred and fifty-three fish: 'an all-round perfect number'; 'one of each known species, symbolising the universal gospel' (Jerome); there are said to be one hundred and fifty-three explanations! Any angler would explain, with exaggerated patience, that the fisherman was not yet born who did not count his catch, especially if it was to be divided.

The promise, or warning, that Peter's hitherto unfettered weakness (18) would yet rise to a noble martyrdom was, for such as Peter, a word of encouragement. He would succeed at last. To 'stretch out the hands' was a familiar euphemism for crucifixion; 'another will gird you' (with bonds, to a cross?) glances back to 7. John apparently knows that Peter has so died, and pays a fitting tribute in 19. (See also commentary on 1:41–42.)

An explanation   *John 21:20–23*

At 20 the postscript turns neatly to its second purpose, the correction
of a current misunderstanding. 'The beloved disciple' is introduced
again (see comentary on 13:23–26), and his close relation to Jesus
deliberately recalled, as prelude to a natural enquiry from Peter about
his friend's future—would he also suffer martyrdom? The form of
Jesus' reply had through the intervening years given rise to the belief
that the beloved disciple would live until the advent.

Evidently he had now died, and some in the Church were perplexed
at the contradiction of Jesus' supposed promise. John explains that
Jesus made no such statement, he merely posited a possibility, evading
Peter's question and warning him (in effect) to 'mind his own
business'. The incident was unimportant until misunderstanding
arose, but the absolute right of the risen Lord to dispose of each
disciple's future as he chooses, without answering to others, or
comparisons with others, needed to be affirmed. It still does.

Someone's comment   *John 21:24–25*

There the book abruptly ends, except for a second 'tail-piece', one
which raises more questions than it answers. (See our introductory
paragraphs, 'Why doubt the tradition?') 'These things' in verse 24 could
refer only to the things just recorded (21–23), lending weight to the
correction of current opinion. Alternatively, it could refer to the whole
of chapter 21. However carefully the language of this chapter is
analysed, it remains uncertain whether it was written by the author
of the book or by a later 'editor'. On the whole it seems more probable
that 'these things' refer to the whole book. We wish we knew who these
believers were who support the testimony of the 'witness'. We wish
even more that we knew who that witness was, who needed such
anonymous commendation.

And who is the 'I' of 25, who echoes 20:30, and employs an
engaging exaggeration to convey his wondering admiration of Jesus?
(X-ray examination of erasure at the end of one—only one—ancient
manuscript copy, suggests that 25 is the comment of a later copyist
who has just completed the four Gospels, his hand weary, his eyes
sore, but his heart swelling with devotion to such a Lord!)

A pleasant fancy, of course. But somehow fitting. What a book John
has bequeathed to us! What striking sayings: 'In the beginning was the
Word ... In him was life ... The Word became flesh and dwelt among
us ... God so loved the world that he gave us his only Son ... the Saviour
of the world ... I am the bread of life ... the light of the world ... the

faithful shepherd ... the resurrection and the life ... He that has the Son has life ... Except I wash you, you have no part in me ... Behold the lamb of God ... I will not leave you orphans, I will come to you ... [The Spirit] dwells with you and shall be in you ... My Lord and my God!'

And what dramatic scenes: a secret, midnight conversation with a Rabbi ... an encounter with a lone woman at the well ... a marvellous picnic ... a disturbance at the Feast of Tabernacles ... Jesus before the tomb of Lazarus ... and on his knees, washing the disciples' feet ... Jesus in Pilate's judgment hall ... and on Golgotha ... and meeting Mary in the garden ... and gently confronting doubting Thomas ... and calling to his 'lads' across the lake ...

And all written that we might believe that Jesus is the Christ, the Son of God, and that believing we might have life in his name.

Suggestions for group discussion:

1   What striking phrases or dramatic scenes from John's Gospel would each member of the group in turn add to our final paragraphs, and why?

2   'The absolute right of the risen Lord to dispose of each disciple's future as he chooses, without answering to others ... Others may, you may not; others must, but you need not ...' Does the group approve of this individualist view of Christian discipleship?

3   In the Eastern Orthodox churches, John's emphasis upon incarnation, eternal life, resurrection and union with God, has been accorded pre-eminence, rather than (as in the West) Paul's emphasis upon belief, atonement, forgiveness of sins, and the law of love. Does the group envy the Eastern emphasis?

Merciful Lord, we beseech thee to cast thy bright beams of light upon thy Church, that it being enlightened by the doctrine of thy blessed Apostle and Evangelist Saint John may so walk in the light of thy truth, that it may at length attain to the light of everlasting life; through Jesus Christ our Lord. Amen.

Book of Common Prayer

Further Reading

A.M. Hunter, *According to John*, SCM Press
F.F. Bruce, *St John*, Pickering and Inglis
R.G.V. Tasker, *John*, Tyndale Commentary, Inter-Varsity Press
William Barclay, *Daily Study Bible: St John*, St Andrew Press

For more advanced study

C.K. Barrett, *The Gospel According to St John*, SPCK
John Marsh, *The Gospel of St John*, Pelican Commentary, Penguin
Barnabas Lindars, *The Gospel of John*, New Century Bible, Marshall